CONTENTS

WHAT I

Ever since the end of the Edo Period, when the Japanese started making sushi rolls with motifs for festive occasions, hundreds of variations have been created in all parts of the country. Hana Sushi literally means "floral sushi", but now it seems to include all kinds of artistic sushi that have a decorative-and edible-motif.

Notes for Illustrations

HANA SUSHI can be rolled in two different methods:

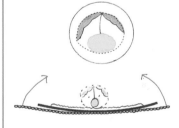

1. Spread rice thinly over *nori*, arrange fillings, and then roll up. The dotted circle indicates that the inner cylinder that is wrapped in the spread rice.

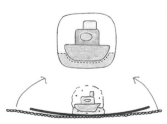

2. Make a mound of rice in the center of *nori* to serve as a base for fillings. Stack and shape fillings into a cylinder, and then wrap up with *nori*. The lower dotted line indicates that a mound of rice is formed under it, as the base for the whole cylinder or log.

BASIC HANA SUSHI

Feast for the eye, as well as the palate, these lovely pink sushi rolls will be a loving gift to your guests around the table.

TYPICAL FLOWER MOTIFS

CHERRY BLOSSOM

Makes 1 roll
2-2½ cups vinegared rice (p 86)
3 sheets toasted nori
***Sakura dembu* (cod flakes)**
2 tsps *tobiko* (salted flying fish roe)

1. In a bowl, fold *sakura dembu* into ⅓ of the vinegared rice, using a rice paddle until evenly tinted. Set aside.
2. Cut 2 sheets of *nori* across the length, into 2½" (6 cm) wide strips. Over one strip laid on bamboo mat, place colored rice from side to side. Fold the mat tightly and press ends to form a teardrop shape.
3. Make 4 more "petals." Assemble petals, filling any gaps between the petals with a small amount of the white rice, to form a cylinder.
4. Spread and press the remaining rice evenly on the full sheet of *nori*, and place the flower on it. Roll up tightly.
5. Slice and decorate each flower center with a mound of *tobiko*.

Note: For more detailed instructions, see p 4.

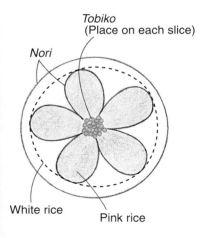

Tobiko
(Place on each slice)

Nori

White rice

Pink rice

PEACH BLOSSOM

Makes 1 roll
2-2½ cups vinegared rice (p 86)
3 sheets toasted *nori*
***Sakura dembu* (cod flakes)**
2-3 sticks *yamagobo* pickles (pokeweed)

1. In a bowl, fold *sakura dembu* into ⅓ of the vinegared rice until evenly tinted. Set aside.
2. Cut 2 sheets of *nori*, across the length, into 3" (7.5 cm) wide strips. Over one strip, place colored rice from side to side. Fold and press ends to form a teardrop shape (p 4). Make 5.
3. Assemble 5 petals around the *yamagobo* root, filling in gaps with pressed white rice, to form a cylinder.
4. Spread and press the remaining rice evenly over the full sheet of *nori*, and center the flower "log." Roll up tightly and slice.

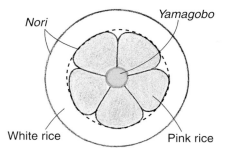

DOUBLE CHERRY

Makes 1 roll
2-2½ cups vinegared rice (p 86)
3 sheets toasted *nori*
***Sakura dembu* (cod flakes)**
***Tamagoyaki* (thick omelet - p 69), julienned**

1. In a bowl, fold *sakura dembu* into ⅓ of the rice until evenly tinted. Set aside.
2. Cut 2 sheets of *nori*, across the length into 2½ " (6 cm) wide strips. Over one strip, spread the colored rice from side to side. Fold in half using the mat, sandwiching a sliced omelet, and press ends to form a teardrop shape (p 4). Make 6.
3. Assemble 6 petals, filling in any gap between the petals with a small portion of pressed white rice, to form a cylinder.
4. Spread and press the remaining rice evenly over the full sheet of *nori*, and center the flower "log." Roll up tightly and slice.

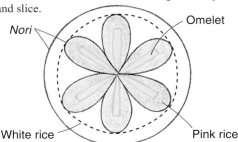

HOW TO ROLL BASIC HANA SUSHI

Makes 1 roll
2-2½ cups vinegared rice (p 86)
3 sheets toasted *nori*
2-3 Tbsps *sakura dembu* (cod flakes)
2 tsps *tobiko* (salted flying fish roe)

Preparation: Fold *sakura dembu* into ⅓ of the vinegared rice, and set aside.

Cut *nori*, across its length, into 2½"(6 cm) strips. Lay one strip on a bamboo mat, and spread ⅕ of the pink rice, leaving ⅜"(1cm) of *nori* at each edge.

Fold it in half, using the bamboo mat. Press edges together to form a petal shape.

Make 4 more "petals."

Spread a moistened thin kitchen cloth over the bamboo mat, and hold it in your hand. Place one of the petals, and add a little rice to its sides, pressing evenly.

Join another "petal." Repeat by adding a little rice as an adhesive, so that the petals radiate from the center. Hold the bamboo mat in a desired arch.

All five petals are assembled into a cylinder of flower.

Lay the bamboo mat, place a full sheet of *nori*, shiny side down, aligning near edges.

Spread rice evenly, leaving 1" (2.5 cm) at the far edge of *nori* uncovered.

Center the flower roll.

Lift up near edge of the mat, and start rolling.

Check if the flower roll is thick enough. Add more rice if necessary, before sealing the *nori*. It is important to pack the rice well so that the flower stays in place.

12

Roll up and press to tighten the roll.

13

Be sure to form a perfect cylinder.

14

Press ends to flatten the rice, with wetted fingers. Let stand with the joined edge down until it is securely sealed.

NORI SHEET FACTS

Roll up toward the far edge.

7¼" (19 cm) Width

8¼" (21 cm) Length

When cutting a sheet into strips or halves for the recipes, be sure to cut across the length as you need the same width for making both inner and outer rolls.

Tip:
When making sushi rolls with figures, be sure to pack more rice than you usually do for common rolls. If the rice is too loose, the fillings may get out of shape when sliced.

COLORING AND SEASONING RICE

Besides pink rice for the spring flowers, you can add your own touch by using different hues and flavors.

*Pink rice
Use 3 Tbsps of *sakura dembu* (cod flakes) for 1 cup of vinegared rice.
Combine *sakura dembu* and the rice. Use a plastic rice paddle or wetted wooden rice paddle with a light, slicing motion, so as not to break or crush the rice grains. As *sakura dembu* makes the mixture too wet to roll right away, let stand for 5 minutes until the excess moisture is absorbed.

*Purple rice
Use 2 tsps of *yukari* (*shiso* sprinkles) for 1 cup of vinegared rice.
Combine the rice with *yukari*. Use a plastic rice paddle or wetted wooden paddle with a light, slicing motion, so as not to break or crush the rice grains. Do not use too much *yukari* since the purple color will deepen after a while as the dry sprinkles spread out into the moisture of the rice.

*Yellow rice
Use 3 Tbsps of egg *soboro* for 1 cup of vinegared rice.
Combine the rice with egg *soboro*. Use a plastic rice paddle or wetted wooden paddle with a light, slicing motion, so as not to break or crush rice grains.

Egg *soboro*
4 whole eggs, beaten
2 egg yolks
4 Tbsps water
2 Tbsps sugar
Salt
Vegetable oil
Combine eggs, egg yolks, water and sugar well. Heat oil in a frying pan, and stir in the egg mixture. Holding 4-5 chopsticks, stir vigorously until finely crumbled. Remove from the pan immediately.

Note: For a brighter yellow, use egg yolks that are boiled and strained through a sifter.

MORE HINTS FOR COLORING

Combine 1 cup vinegared rice with each of the following:

*Green: 1 Tbsp *aonori* (green seaweed sprinkles)

*Red: 2 oz (60 g) *tarako* (salted cod roe)

*Beige: 1 Tbsp toasted white sesame seeds

*Pale pink: 2 Tbsps cooked salmon flakes

*Black: 2 Tbsps toasted black sesame seeds

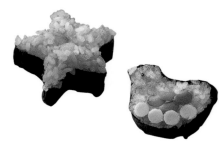

DANDELION

Makes 1 roll
2-2½ cups vinegared rice (p 86)
2 sheets toasted *nori*
Egg *soboro* (p 5)
1 oz (30g) pickled greens
 (such as *takana* or *nozawana*)

1. Make yellow rice by combining ⅙ of the rice with the egg *soboro*.
2. Place a sheet of *nori* on a bamboo mat, and spread the white rice evenly over it, leaving 1"(2.5 cm) at the far edge.
3. Place the yellow rice in the center from side to side, pressing firmly to form a cylinder.
4. Cut two 2"(5 cm) wide strips of *nori*. Fold each into a "V ," and join them to shape stem and leaves. Stuff the concaves with the rice. Place it upside down over the yellow cylinder, pressing gently to form a larger cylinder.
5. Place pickled greens along the outside of *nori*, on both sides.
6. Lift near and far edges of the mat, join them in your hands to wrap up tightly into a roll. Overlap the ends of *nori* to secure.

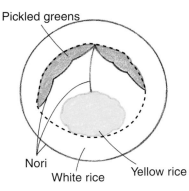

Pickled greens

Nori

White rice

Yellow rice

FUN PATTERNS

Season's transition, good old design motifs, cute animals or fruits around you ... you can redesign any charming sight for this type of sushi. Be imaginative and create your own motifs.

TULIP

Makes 1 roll
2-2½ cups vinegared rice (p 86)
2 sheets toasted *nori*
1½ fish sausage or hot dog
1 Japanese cucumber

1. Cut 2 notches into the sausage, lengthwise, to shape the top part of tulip. Slice the cucumber lengthwise, keeping the skin. Taper sides using a peeler. Make 2.
2. Place a sheet of *nori* on a bamboo mat, and spread ⅘ of the rice evenly, leaving 2"(5 cm) from the far edge. Place 2 cucumber strips in the center.
3. Cut two 2"(5 cm) wide strips of *nori*, and fold each lengthwise in half to form a "V ." Join them to shape stem and leaves, and place on the cucumber. Fill any gaps with pressed rice.
4. Place the sausage on it, and fill in any gaps with rice, forming into a thick cylinder.
5. Lift near and far edges of the mat, join them in your hands to wrap up tightly into a roll. Overlap the end of *nori* to secure.

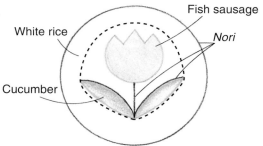

ZINNIA

Makes 1 roll
2-2½ cups vinegared rice (p 86)
3 sheets toasted *nori*
1 Japanese cucumber, sliced lengthwise
***Sakura dembu* (cod flakes)**
Egg *soboro* (p 5)

1. Make pink rice by folding *sakura dembu* into ⅙ of the rice. Make yellow rice by combining a little amount of the rice and egg *soboro*.
2. Cut three 2"(5 cm) wide strips of *nori*. Place 1 strip on a bamboo mat, and roll up the yellow rice. Cut a 3½ "(9 cm) wide strip of *nori* (save two for later), and place on the mat. Spread the pink rice over it, center the yellow rice cylinder, and roll up tightly.
3. Place a full sheet of *nori* on a bamboo mat. Spread the rice evenly, leaving 2"(5 cm) at the far edge. Lay cucumber strips in the center. Fold 2 narrow strips of *nori* in half lengthwise to form a "V". Join them to shape stem and leaves, and place on the cucumber. Fill the concaves with pressed rice.
4. Place the "flower" cylinder. Form a thicker cylinder by filling in any gaps firmly with the rice. Join the edges of the mat in your hands into a tight roll. Overlap the end of *nori* to secure.

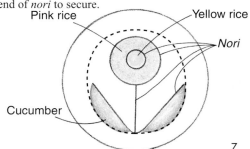

SHIP

Makes 1 roll
2½ cups vinegared rice (p 86)
3 sheets toasted *nori*
***Tobiko* (salted flying fish roe)**
***Sakura dembu* (cod flakes)**
***Aonori* (green seaweed sprinkles)**
Egg *soboro* (p 5)

1. Combine ½ cup each vinegared rice with *tobiko* for orange rice, and with *aonori* for green rice. Make pink rice by combining ⅓ cup vinegared rice with *sakura dembu*, and yellow rice by mixing a little rice with egg *soboro*.
2. Cut a 4¾"(12 cm) wide strip out of a full sheet of *nori* (cut across the length), and wrap the orange rice in, pressing into a vessel form.
3. Cut two 1½"(4 cm) wide strips of *nori* (save 1 for later), and roll up the yellow rice into a cylinder.
4. On a 3"(8 cm) strip of *nori*, place pink rice and center the yellow rice cylinder; roll up and form a square log.
5. Using another 1½"(4 cm) strip of *nori*, roll a tiny square log of green rice.
6. Lay a full sheet of *nori* on a bamboo mat. Mound some of the green rice, then orange, pink, and green logs.
7. Fill in any gaps with white rice, gently pressing to form a thick cylinder.
8. Lift both edges of the mat, join them in your

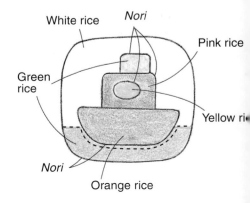

White rice
Nori
Pink rice
Green rice
Yellow ri[ce]
Nori
Orange rice

SAILBOAT

Makes 1 roll
2-2½ cups vinegared rice (p 86)
2 sheets toasted *nori*
***Aonori* (green seaweed sprinkles)**
***Yukari* (*shiso* sprinkles)**
***Tamagoyaki* (thick omelet - p 69)**

1. Make green rice by combining ⅓ of the rice with *aonori*.
Make a small amount of purple rice with *yukari*.
2. Cut two 3½"(9 cm) wide strips of *nori*. Make "sail" by
wrapping purple rice in one strip. Wrap the other *nori* around the
omelet cut into a trapezoid log.
3. Lay a full sheet of *nori* on a bamboo mat. Mound some of the
green rice in the center, and place the wrapped omelet on it.
Standing the "sail" on its tip, fill any gaps with pressed white
rice, and form into a thick cylinder.
4. Lift near and far edges of the mat, wrap with *nori* by joining
both edges of mat held in your hands.

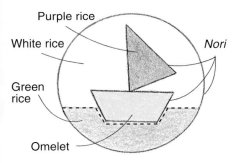

Purple rice
White rice
Nori
Green rice
Omelet

BALLOON

Makes 1 roll
2- 2½ cups vinegared rice (p 86)
3 sheets toasted *nori*
Egg *soboro* (p 5)
Cucumber stick

1. Make yellow rice by combining ⅓ of the
vinegared rice with egg *soboro*.
2. Cut a 4 ¾"(12 cm) strip of *nori*, and wrap in
gently pressed yellow rice, forming a cylinder.
3. Wrap 2 ½"(6 cm) strip of *nori* around the cucumber
stick.
4. Lay a full sheet of *nori* on a bamboo mat. Spread
the white rice (save some for later) over it, and
center the yellow "balloon". Put a bit of rice on it,
and attach two 1" (2.5 cm) strips of *nori* to its sides.
5. Plaee the wrapped cucumber. Adding more rice, form a
cylinder.
6. Lift near and far edges of the mat, join them in
your hands to wrap up tightly into a roll. Overlap the
ends of *nori* to secure.

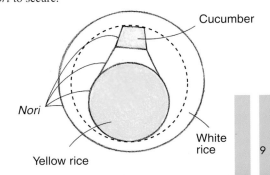

Cucumber
Nori
Yellow rice
White rice

9

SWIRL

Makes 1 roll
1½- 2 cups vinegared rice (p 86)
1 sheet toasted *nori*
Sakura dembu (cod flakes),
Tobiko (salted flying fish roe), Egg *soboro* (p 5)
Aonori (green seaweed sprinkles), *Yukari* (*shiso* sprinkles)

1. Divide the rice into 5. Combine each portion with *sakura dembu*, *tobiko*, egg *soboro*, *aonori* and *yukari* to make five colors. Make pink rice first and let it stand until excess moisture is absorbed.
2. Over the full sheet of *nori* placed on a bamboo mat, spread colored rice portions in order: pink, orange, yellow, green and purple, beginning from the near edge and ending with less grains of rice.
3. Lift the near edge of the mat, and press the pink rice inside. Lift away the mat, and start rolling. Secure the ends.

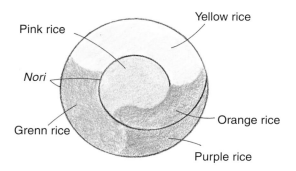

Pink rice
Yellow rice
Nori
Grenn rice
Orange rice
Purple rice

MITSUDOMOE (TRICOLOR SWIRL)

Makes 1 roll
2-2½ cups vinegared rice (p 86)
3 sheets toasted *nori*
Sakura dembu (cod flakes), Egg *soboro* (p 5)
Aonori (green seaweed sprinkles),
Yukari (*shiso* sprinkles)
2-3 sticks *yamagobo* pickles (pokeweed)
Pickled greens (such as *mibuna* or *nozawana*)

1. Divide the rice into 3 portions. Combine 1 portion with *sakura dembu*, and set aside. Combine each remaining portion with egg *soboro* and with *aonori*.
2. Cut a full sheet of *nori* in half across the length. Over a half sheet, spread the yellow rice, and center the *yamagobo* root. Fold the *nori* to form a teardrop. In the same manner, make a pink teardrop with pickled greens center, and a green teardrop with *yukari* center. See page 4 for shaping.
3. Assemble the three so they interlock each other, and shape into a cylinder using a bamboo mat.
4. Place a full sheet of *nori* on a bamboo mat, and roll up the cylinder tightly.

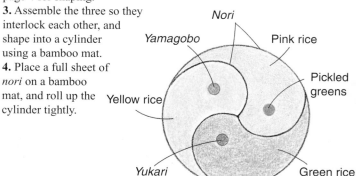

Nori
Pink rice
Yamagobo
Pickled greens
Yellow rice
Yukari
Green rice

TRADITIONAL PATTERNS FOR FESTIVE OCCASIONS

These smart designs have been used widely in Japan as old family crests to be displayed on *kimonos*, tools or as roof tile decorations. These rolls are fun to look at and also to taste because they pack three to five different flavors in one slice.

YOTSUME (FOUR SQUARES)

Makes 1 roll
2-2½ cups vinegared rice (p 86)
3 sheets toasted *nori*
Sakura dembu (cod flakes)
Tobiko (salted flying fish roe)
Egg *soboro* (p 5)
Yukari (*shiso* sprinkles)
Yamagobo pickles (pokeweed)
Pickled greens (*mibuna* or *nozawana*)
Tamagoyaki (thick omelet - p 69)

1. Divide the rice into quarters. Make pink rice by combining one portion of the rice with *sakura dembu*, and set aside. Make orange rice with *tobiko*, yellow rice with omelet, and purple rice with *yukari* in the same manner.
2. Cut a full sheet of *nori* into half across the length, and place on a bamboo mat. Spread and press the pink rice and center the *yukari*. Folding the mat, form a fan shape. In the same manner, make an orange roll with pickled greens center, a yellow roll with *yamagobo* center, and a purple roll with an omelet stick.
3. Assemble the four "fans" to form a log, using the mat.
4. Place a full sheet of *nori* on the mat, and roll up the log.

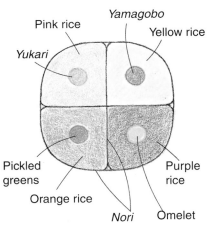

Pink rice
Yamagobo
Yellow rice
Yukari
Pickled greens
Orange rice
Nori
Omelet
Purple rice

SNOWMAN

Makes 1 roll
2-2½ cups vinegared rice (p 86)
3 sheets toasted *nori*
**2-3 sticks *yamagobo* pickles
  (pokeweed)**
Cucumber, julienned

1. Roll some of the pressed rice in a half sheet of *nori*, into an oval roll. Make 2 for body.
2. Wrap *yamagobo* with a 1½"(4 cm) strip of *nori*.
3. Lay a full sheet of nori on a bamboo mat. Spread the rice (save some for later) over it. Place "snowman" in the center, and fill any gaps with the remaining rice, shaping into a tight cylinder. Top with *yamagobo* and a thin cucumber strip.
4. Lift near and far edges of the mat, join them in your hands to wrap up tightly into a roll. Overlap the ends of *nori* to secure.

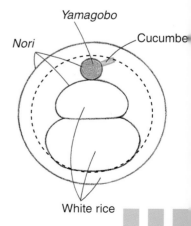

Yamagobo

Nori

Cucumbe

White rice

PARTY BALLOONS

Makes 1 roll
2-2½ cups vinegared rice (p 86)
2 sheets toasted *nori*
***Sakura dembu* (cod flakes), Egg *soboro* (p 5), *Yukari* (*shiso* sprinkles)**
2-3 sticks *yamagobo* pickles (pokeweed)

1. Mix a small amount of the rice with *sakura dembu* to make pink rice, and set aside. Mix the same amount of the rice with egg *soboro* to make yellow rice. In the same manner, make purple rice with *yukari*.
2. Cut three 3"(8 cm) strips of *nori*, and make three "teardrops" with three different colors. See page 4 for shaping.
3. Assemble the three, by sticking them with some rice as shown, including *yamagobo* root. Shape into a log.
4. Lay a full sheet of *nori* on a bamboo mat. Spread the white rice over it and center the log.
5. Lift near and far edges of the mat, join them in your hands to wrap up tightly into a roll. Overlap the ends of *nori* to secure.

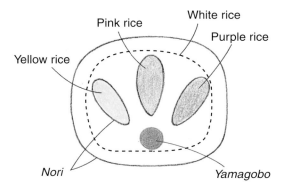

Pink rice
White rice
Purple rice
Yellow rice
Nori
Yamagobo

Makes 1 roll
2-2½ cups vinegared rice (p 86)
3 sheets toasted *nori*
***Yukari* (*shiso* sprinkles)**
***Sakura dembu* (cod flakes)**

1. Make a small amount of pink rice by mixing the rice and *sakura dembu*, and set aside. In the same manner, make purple rice with *yukari*.
2. Cut a 3 ½"(9 cm) wide strip of *nori*, and roll purple rice into a square log using the mat.
3. Cut a 3"(8 cm) wide strip of *nori*, and roll pink rice into a triangular log, leaving the end of *nori* free for "tail".
4. Lay a full sheet of *nori* on a bamboo mat. Spread the white rice (save some for later) all over it. Stand a very thin strip of *nori* in the center to make stem, and secure it with some of the saved rice, pressing from the sides.
5. Place the purple log, then the pink one on the stem, and fill any gaps with the remaining rice to form a cylinder.
6. Lift near and far edges of the mat, join them in your hands to wrap up tightly into a roll. Overlap the ends of *nori* to secure.

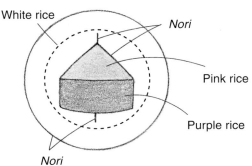

White rice
Nori
Pink rice
Purple rice
Nori

ACORN

BUNNY

Makes 1 roll
2½ -3 cups vinegared rice (p 86)
4 sheets toasted *nori*
***Sakura dembu* (cod flakes)**
Simmered *kampyo* (p 82)

1. Fold *sakura dembu* into ⅘ of the rice evenly to make pink rice, and set aside until excess moisture is absorbed.
2. Cut three 1"(2.5 cm) wide strips of *nori*. Make sticks of eyes and nose by wrapping the *nori* around narrow strips of *kampyo*. Make mouth by wrapping a 3"(8 cm) strip of *nori* around a wider strip of *kampyo*.
3. Lay a full sheet of *nori* on a bamboo mat. Mound some of the pink rice in the center. Position eyes, nose and mouth, filling the gaps with the remaining rice, and form into a cylinder. Lift near and far edges of the mat, and join them in your hands.
4. Make ears. Cut a 4"(10 cm) strip of *nori*, place a small amount of the white rice on it, and roll into an oval log. Cut a 6"(15 cm) strip of *nori*, spread the remaining pink rice over it, and place the oval log; roll up.
5. Cut the oval log in half, and stick to the bunny's head.

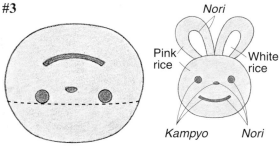

#3

14

Makes 1 roll
2½-3 cups vinegared rice (p 86)
3 sheets toasted *nori*
Simmered *kampyo* (p 82)
2½ Tbsps white sesame seeds, toasted
1 Tbsp *katsuobushi* (dried bonito shavings)
Dash soy sauce

1. Combine the *katsuobushi* and ½ Tbsp sesame seeds with soy sauce just enough to moisten the mixture. Combine a quarter of the rice with this to make brown rice until evenly mixed. Combine the remaining rice with 2 Tbsps sesame seeds to make beige rice.
2. Make eyes and nose. Cut three 1"(2.5 cm) strips of *nori*, and wrap each around a thin strip of *kampyo*. Make 2 for eyes, 1 for mouth.
3. Cut three 4"(10 cm) strips of *nori*. With one strip, roll up brown rice and one "eye."
4. Lay a full sheet of *nori* on a bamboo mat. Mound some of the beige rice in the center. Position eyes, then nose, filling the gaps with beige rice to form a tightly packed cylinder. Lift near and far edges of the mat, and join them in your hands.
5. On one remaining strip of *nori*, place brown rice and form a teardrop log, leaving one edge of the *nori* loose. Form another teardrop with beige rice. Stick these "ears" to the head.

FLOPPY EAR DOG

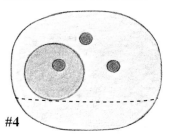

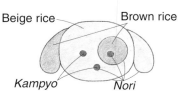

Beige rice — Brown rice
Kampyo — *Nori*

#4

BEAR

Makes 1 roll
2½-3 cups vinegared rice (p 86)
3 sheets toasted *nori*
Egg *soboro* (p 5)
White sesame seeds, toasted
Simmered *kampyo* (p 82)

1. Fold egg *soboro* into half portion of the rice to make yellow rice. Fold sesame seeds into half of the remaining portion of the rice to make ears.
2. Cut three 1"(2.5 cm) strips of *nori*. Wrap each around a thin strip of *kampyo*. Make 2 for eyes and 1 for nose.
3. On a 5" (13 cm) strip of *nori* placed on the mat, place "nose" strip, and spread the remaining white rice. Roll up to make muzzle.
4. Lay a full sheet of *nori* on a bamboo mat. Mound some of the yellow rice in the center, and position eyes on it. Add some more yellow rice, and then place "muzzle." Lift near and far edges of the mat, and join them in your hands.
5. Make ears. Cut a sheet of *nori* in half across the length, and place the beige rice in the center. Roll up into an oval and cut lengthwise into halves. Stick them to the head.

Note: See page 17 for step-by-step instructions.

#4

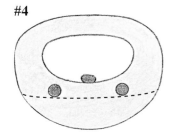

Beige rice
Nori — *Kampyo*
Yellow rice — White rice

15

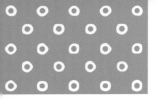

BEAR

Crunchy, *tobiko* rice makes the face of the bear while the ears are made of soy sauce and bonito flavored rice. *Kampyo* gives accents not only as the features but also tastewise.

#7

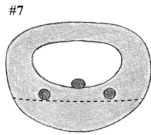

Brown rice　　*Kampyo*

White rice

Nori　　Orange rice

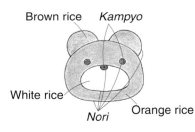

16

HOW TO ROLL ANIMAL SUSHI

Makes 1 roll
2½-3 cups vinegared rice (p 86)
3 sheets toasted *nori*
***Tobiko* (salted flying fish roe)**
Simmered *kampyo* **(p 82)**
½ Tbsp white sesame seeds, toasted
1 Tbsp *katsuobushi* **(dried bonito shavings)**
Dash soy sauce

Preparation: Combine *katsuobushi* and sesame seeds with soy sauce just enough to moisten the mixture. Combine a quarter of the rice with this until evenly mixed. Combine half of the remaining rice with *tobiko* to make orange rice.

1 Make eyes and nose. Cut three 1" (2.5 cm) strips of *nori*, and wrap each around three strips of thinly cut *kampyo*.

2 Make muzzle. Place a wrapped *kampyo* in the center of 6"(15 cm) wide strip of *nor*i on a bamboo mat, and spread the white rice over it.

3 Using the mat, shape into an oval roll.

4 Make face. Lay a full sheet of *nori* on a bamboo mat. Mound some of the orange rice, and position 2 strips of wrapped *kampyo* apart.

5 Cover with some of the orange rice. Place muzzle on it.

6 Coat the whole with orange rice to form into a cylinder. Lift the mat and wrap halfway.

7 Lift the far edge of the mat to wrap up tightly into a roll. Press gently to form an oval cylinder.

8 Make ears. Place the brown rice in the center of a half sheet of *nori*.

9 Roll up and shape into an oval.

10 Cut in half lengthwise.

11 Stick them, rice side down, to the bear head.

KITTEN

Makes 1 roll
2½-3 cups vinegared rice (p 86)
3 sheets toasted *nori*
Egg *soboro* (p 5)
Simmered *kampyo* (p 82)

1. Make yellow rice by folding egg *soboro* into the rice until evenly tinted.
2. Place a thinly cut *kampyo* strip in the center of 3"(8 cm) strip of *nori*. Fold the *nori* in half, and leave the ends separate to form muzzle. Cut two 2 ½"(6 cm) strips of *nori*, and wrap around thinly cut *kampyo* strips to make eyes.
3. Lay a full sheet of *nori* on a bamboo mat. Mound some of the yellow rice in the center, and position eyes on it. Cover them with a little rice, then position muzzle. Add more rice (save some for ears) and form a cylinder.
4. Lift near and far edges of the mat, and join them in your hands.
5. Make ears. On a half sheet of *nori*, place the remaining rice and roll into a diamond log. Cut into halves lengthwise, and stick them to the head.

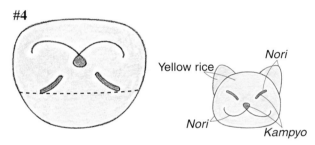

PIGLET

Makes 1 roll
2-2½ cups vinegared rice (p 86)
4 sheets toasted *nori*
Salmon flakes
Simmered *kampyo* (p 82)

1. Make pink rice by folding salmon flakes into the rice.
2. Make eyes by wrapping two 1"(2.5 cm) strips of *nori* around two strips of thin *kampyo* strips.
3. Make nostrils by rolling little rice with two 2 ½"(6 cm) strips of *nori*.
4. Make muzzle. Spread the rice on a 6"(15 cm) strip of *nori* placed on the mat, and position nostrils; roll up tightly.
5. Make ears. Cut two 3"(8 cm) strips of *nori*, and roll little rice in each.
6. Lay a full sheet of *nori* on a bamboo mat. Mound some of the pink rice, and position ears on its sides. Adding rice to fill any gaps, position eyes and muzzle, forming a thick cylinder. Lift near and far edges of the mat, and join them in your hands.

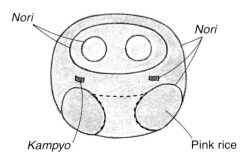

PANDA BEAR

Makes 1 roll
2½-3 cups vinegared rice (p 86)
3 sheets toasted *nori*
Toasted black sesame seeds
Simmered *kampyo* (p 82)

1. Fold black sesame seeds into ⅓ of the rice until evenly mixed.

2. Make nose by wrapping a 1"(2.5 cm) strip of *nori* around a *kampyo* strip.

3. Make eye circles. On a 3"(8 cm) strip of *nori*, place some black rice, and position a rounded thin strip of *nori* as an eye. Cover with some more rice, and roll up. Make 2. Save the black rice for ears.

4. Lay a full sheet of *nori* on a bamboo mat. Mound some of the white rice in the center. Position nose and eye circles, filling any gaps with white rice. When a thick cylinder is formed, lift near and far edges of the mat, and join them in your hands.

5. Make ears.Roll black rice with a half sheet of *nori*. Cut into halves lengthwise, and stick to the head.

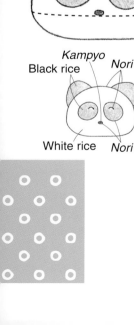

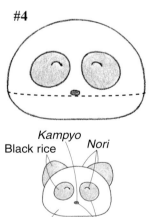

19

WHALE

Makes 1 roll
2-2½ cups vinegared rice (p 86)
2 sheets toasted *nori*
Toasted black sesame seeds

1. Make black rice by combining a quarter of the rice with black sesame seeds.
2. Make whale body by wrapping a 7"(18 cm) strip of *nori* around the black rice, forming whale body.
3. Lay a full sheet of *nori* on a bamboo mat. Spread the white rice (save some for later) all over it. Place whale body on it. Add some more rice, and position a 1½"(4 cm) strip of *nori* folded into V-shape. Filling any gaps with white rice, form a packed, thick cylinder.
4. Lift near and far edges of the mat, and join them in your hands to wrap up tightly. Overlap the ends of *nori* to secure.

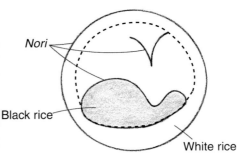

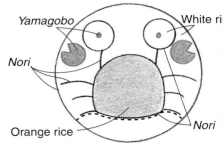

CRAB

Makes 1 roll
2½ cups vinegared rice (p 86)
3 sheets toasted nori
Tobiko **(salted flying fish roe)**
2-3 sticks *yamagobo* pickles (pokeweed)

1. Make orange rice by folding *tobiko* into a quarter of the rice.
2. Cut a 5"(13 cm) strip of *nori*, and roll the orange rice for "body."
3. Make eyes. On a 3"(8 cm) strip of *nori*, spread little rice, and center julienned *yamagobo* root; roll up. Make two and set aside.
4. Lay a full sheet of *nori* on a bamboo mat. Spread the white rice (save some for later) all over it, and position six ¾"(2 cm) strips of *nori* on both sides of the rice. Place body in the center, and add little rice onto the sides. Layer thin strips of *nori* and rice to form legs. Add some rice on the body, and set two "claws" of notched *yamagobo* at the sides.
5. Stand 2 thin strips of *nori* (½"/1.5 cm) on the sides of the body, holding it with rice, and position eyes. Fill any gaps with some more rice, and form a thick cylinder.
6. Lift near and far edges of the mat, and join them in your hands.

SEA TURTLE

Makes 1 roll
2½ cups vinegared rice (p 86)
3 sheets toasted *nori*
***Aonori* (green seaweed sprinkles)**
Egg *soboro* (p 5)
***Tamagoyaki* (thick omelet - p69)**
Simmered *kampyo* (p 82)
Fish sausage or hot dog
Toasted black sesame seeds

1. Fold *aonori* into a quarter of the rice to make green rice. Fold egg *soboro* into ⅓ of the remaining rice to make yellow rice.
2. Cut a 5"(13 cm) strip of *nori*, roll up green rice in it, and form a tunnel.
3. Cut a 4"(10 cm) strip of *nori*, and roll up the yellow rice in it to make head.
4. Cut a 3"(8 cm) strip of *nori*, and wrap it around the omelet cut into thin strips. Make 2 for feet.
5. Lay a full sheet of *nori* on a bamboo mat. Mound some of the white rice in the center on it. Set feet on it, and fill any gaps with the rice. Place the turtle body and head, and add the remaining rice to form a thick cylinder.
6. Lift near and far edges of the mat, and join them in your hands.
7. Slice, and place a black sesame seed on each slice as an eye.

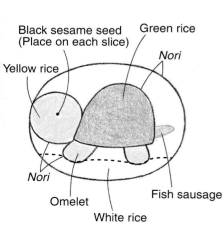

Black sesame seed
(Place on each slice)   Green rice
Yellow rice   *Nori*

Nori
        Omelet   Fish sausage
              White rice

GRAPES

Flavorful, *yukari* rice is rolled up as thinly as possible to form the grape cluster. Make at least six grapes for one roll. It is a challenge, but is worth the effort.

APPLE

The fruit is made of red rice made of *tarako*, or salted cod roe. A tiny young leaf made of cucumber is added as a finishing touch.

CHERRIES

The key to success is separating the cherries.

GRAPES

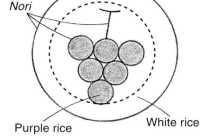

Nori · Purple rice · White rice

Makes 1 roll
2-2½ cups vinegared rice (p 86)
3 sheets toasted *nori*
Yukari (*shiso* sprinkles)

1. Combine ⅓ of the rice with *yukari* to make purple rice.
2. Cut six 2 ½"(6 cm) wide strip of *nori*, and place as little rice as possible; roll up. Make 6 or more.
3. Lay a full sheet of *nori* on a bamboo mat. Spread the white rice (save some for later) all over it. Set grape cluster by adding and pressing more rice around it. Stand a 1"(2.5 cm) strip of *nori*, and hold it in place by adding the rice. Fold the same strip of *nori* in half, and add to the top. Add the remaining rice and press into a thick cylinder.
4. Lift near and far edges of the mat, and join them in your hands to wrap up tightly. Overlap the ends of *nori* to secure.

APPLE

Makes 1 roll
2-2½ cups vinegared rice (p 86)
2 sheets toasted *nori*
Tarako (salted cod roe)
Cucumber

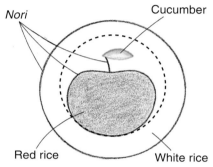

Nori · Cucumber · Red rice · White rice

1. Combine ⅓ of the rice with *tarako* for the fruit.
2. Cut an 8"(15 cm) strip of *nori*, and roll up the red rice, leaving ⅜" (1 cm) of its end loose for stem.
3. Lay a full sheet of *nori* on a bamboo mat. Spread the white rice (save some for later) over it, and cover the apple with added rice, holding the stem part of the *nori* in place. Put a narrow strip of cucumber. Cover it with some more rice, and press the whole piece into a thick cylinder.
4. Lift near and far edges of the mat, and join them in your hands. Overlap the ends of *nori* to secure.

CHERRIES

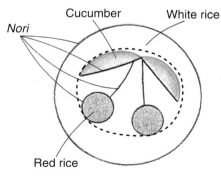

Nori · Cucumber · White rice · Red rice

Makes 1 roll
2-2½ cups vinegared rice (p 86)
3 sheets toasted *nori*
Tarako (salted cod roe)
Cucumber

1. Combine a small amount of the rice with *tarako* for cherries. Slice off two sides of the cucumber .
2. Cut 5"(13 cm) strip of *nori*, and roll up red rice in it, leaving 1"(2.5 cm) from the far edge of *nori* to form stem. Make 2.
3. Lay a full sheet of *nori* on a bamboo mat. Spread the white rice (save some for later) over it. Place two cherries apart. Fold stems in half as shown, and fill any gaps with the rice. Place cucumber strips on each stem. Add more rice and form a thick cylinder. Press firmly.
4. Lift near and far edges of the mat, and join them in your hands tightly. Overlap the ends of *nori* to secure.

TRAIN

This "egg train" with chewy fishcake windows has hot dog pantographs and wheels of *yamagobo* pickles.

Makes 1 roll
1½-2 cups vinegared rice (p 86)
2 sheets toasted *nori*
***Tamagoyaki* (thick omelet - p69)**
***Kamaboko* (fishcake)**
3-4 sticks *yamagobo* pickles (pokeweed)
Fish sausage or hot dog, cut into thin sticks

1. Cut fishcake into eight ¼"(5 mm) sticks. Cut ¾"(2 cm) strip of *nori*, and wrap around 2 fishcake sticks, joined if necessary. Make 4.
2. Cut the omelet into 3 layers, including two ¼"(5 mm) strips for top and middle parts. Cut the middle part into 5 sticks to set the "windows."
3. Lay a full sheet of *nori* on a bamboo mat. Spread the white rice (save some for later) over it. Place *yamagobo* cut in two pieces, apart. Assemble the omelet layers and wrapped fishcake into a train. Stand fish sausage sticks on the point. Fill any gaps with the rice, and form the whole piece into a thick cylinder.
4. Lift near and far edges of the mat, and join them in your hands tightly. Overlap the ends of *nori* to secure.

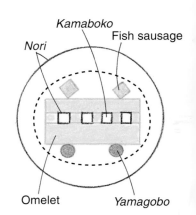

Kamaboko
Fish sausage
Nori
Omelet
Yamagobo

AUTOMOBILE

Makes 1 roll
2-2½ cups vinegared rice (p 86)
3 sheets toasted *nori*
Egg *soboro* (p 5)
Cucumber
Smoked cheese

1. Fold egg *soboro* into ⅓ of the rice to make yellow rice.
2. Split cucumber in two. Cut one half lengthwise into 2 sticks. Wrap each stick with 1½"(4 cm) strip of *nori*. Make 2 for windows.
3. Halve smoked cheese lengthwise, and wrap in 2"(5 cm) strip of *nori*. Make 2 for wheels.
4. Cut an 8"(15 cm) wide *nori*, and place on the mat. Spread some of the yellow rice, then position cucumber windows, and roll up into a vehicle shape.
5. Lay a full sheet of *nori* on a bamboo mat. Spread the white rice (save some for later) over it. Place wheels and body. Filling in any gaps, form the whole piece into a cylinder.
6. Lift near and far edges of the mat, join them in your hands. Overlap the ends of *nori* to secure.

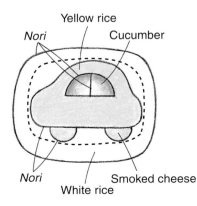

Yellow rice

Nori   Cucumber

Nori

White rice   Smoked cheese

BUTTERFLY

Makes 1 roll
2-2½ cups vinegared rice (p 86)
3 sheets toasted *nori*
Egg *soboro* **(p 5)**
Tamagoyaki **(thick omelet - p69)**
Tobiko **(salted flying fish roe)**

1. Fold egg *soboro* into half of the rice to make yellow rice.
2. Make lower wings. Roll up a little amount of the yellow rice in a 3"(8 cm) strip of *nori*. Make 2.
3. Make upper wings. Roll up half of the remaining yellow rice in a 3½ "(9 cm) strip of *nori*. Make 2.
4. Make feelers by rolling up little amount of the white rice in a 1½"(4 cm) strip of *nori*. Make 2.
5. Lay a full sheet of *nori* on a bamboo mat. Spread the white rice (save some for later) all over it. Place lower wings, standing the egg body in the middle. Place upper wings, then feelers. Fill any gaps with little rice to make a smooth cylinder.
6. Lift near and far edges of the mat, and join them in your hands. Overlap the ends of *nori* to secure.

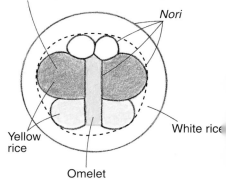

Tobiko (Place on each slice)

Nori

Yellow rice

Omelet

White rice

CHICK

Makes 1 roll
2-2½ cups vinegared rice (p 86)
3 sheets toasted *nori*
Egg *soboro* (p 5)
Boiled carrot
Toasted black sesame seeds

1. Fold egg *soboro* into a quarter of the rice to make yellow rice.
2. Cut a 5"(13 cm) strip of *nori*, and roll up the yellow rice. Using the mat, form a chick shape.
3. Lay a full sheet of *nori* on a bamboo mat. Spread the white rice (save some for later) over it. Place chick body on it, and add more rice around it forming a thick cylinder. Position thinly cut carrot stick as beak, and secure it with little rice.
4. Lift near and far edges of the mat, and join them in your hands. Overlap the ends of *nori* to secure.
5. Slice into 8, and place a sesame seed "eye" on each.

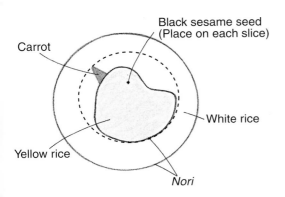

SNAIL

Makes 1 roll
2-2½ cups vinegared rice (p 86)
2 sheets toasted *nori*
***Tobiko* (salted flying fish roe)**
***Tamagoyaki* (thick omelet - p 69)**
***Yamagobo* pickles (pokeweed), julienned**

1. Fold *tobiko* into a quarter of the rice to make orange rice.
2. Cut a 8"(15 cm) strip of *nori*, and spread orange rice. Pressing the near edge of the *nori* onto the rice, and roll up to make "shell."
3. Spread white rice (save some for later) over a full sheet of *nori* placed on the mat. Adding more rice to fill any gaps, position two ¾"(2 cm) strips of *nori* and thin *yamagobo* roots to make feelers.
4. Press the whole piece into a cylinder. Lift near and far edges of the mat, and join them in your hands. Overlap the ends of *nori* to secure.

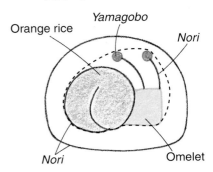

Pine, bamboo and plum form a set of auspicious symbols in Japan,
and simplified motifs such as those shown here have been employed for various celebrations,
including weddings, births and for longevity.

PINE

To form the mounds of pine branch neatly,
add a narrow, half-cut roll on top.

BAMBOO

The key to success is to show the tapered
points of the bamboo leaves and position
them facing different directions.

PLUM BLOSSOM

Mix a generous amount of *sakura dembu*
to make for good color contrast.

PINE

Makes 1 roll
2-2½ cups vinegared rice (p 86)
2 sheets toasted *nori*
***Aonori* (green seaweed sprinkles)**
***Tamagoyaki* (thick omelet - p 69)**

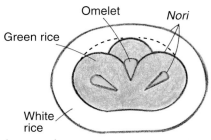

1. Fold *aonori* into half amount of the rice to make green rice.
2. Cut *tamagoyaki* into 3 thin, triangular sticks. Wrap each with a 2½"(6 cm) strip of *nori*.
3. Cut a 3"(8 cm) strip across the length of *nori*, and cut it in half. Using one strip, roll a small amount of the green rice. Cut in half lengthwise. This makes the top of the pine branch.
4. Spread green rice on a 5"(13 cm) strip of *nori*, and position two omelet sticks, filling in any gaps. Bring up the longer sides of *nori* the center, and push in an omelet stick. Place the half-cut roll on top. Add little white rice to the sides of the center mound.
5. Lay a full sheet of *nori* on a bamboo mat. Spread the white rice and place the roll in the center. Lift near and far edges of the mat, and join them in your hands. Form into "bean" shaped log. Overlap the ends of *nori* to secure.

BAMBOO

Makes 1 roll
2-2½ cups vinegared rice (p 86)
3 sheets toasted *nori*
***Aonori* (green seaweed sprinkles)**

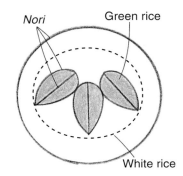

1. Fold *aonori* into ⅓ of the rice. Transfer onto a 2½" (6 cm) strip of *nori* placed on the mat, sandwich a 1"(2.5 cm) strip of *nori*, and fold the mat to form a teardrop log (p 4). Make 3.
2. Lay a full sheet of *nori* on a bamboo mat. Spread the white rice (save some for later) over it. Set three leaves by filling any gaps with white rice.
3. Lift near and far edges of the mat, and join them in your hands. Overlap the ends of *nori* to secure.

PLUM BLOSSOM

Makes 1 roll
2-2½ cups vinegared rice (p 86)
3 sheets toasted *nori*
***Sakura dembu* (cod flakes)**
***Yamagobo* pickles (pokeweed)**

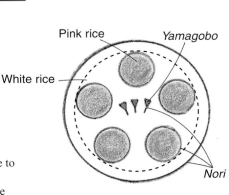

1. Fold *sakura dembu* into a quarter of the rice to make pink rice, and set aside.
2. Cut five 2½"(6 cm) strips of *nori*, and make five thin rolls of pink rice.
3. Cut three 1"(2.5 cm) strips of *nori* and wrap thinly cut *yamagobo* in each.
4. Lay a full sheet of *nori* on a bamboo mat. Spread the white rice (save some) over it, and set the petals and the center by filling any gaps with the remaining rice.
5. Lift near and far edges of the mat, and join them in your hands. Overlap the ends of *nori* to secure.

SMIRKY FACE

Makes 1 roll
2-2½ cups vinegared rice (p 86)
2 sheets toasted *nori*
***Aonori* (green seaweed sprinkles)**
Cucumber, julienned
***Yamagobo* pickles (pokeweed)**
Sliced cooked ham

1. Fold *aonori* into the rice until evenly tinted. Cut the ham into 1"(2.5 cm) strips, and wrap each in a 2 ¾"(7 cm) strip of *nori* to make mouth.
2. Lay a full sheet of *nori* on a bamboo mat. Mound some of the green rice in the center from side to side. Position ham for mouth and thin cucumber sticks for nose, then *yamagobo* roots for eyes, filling any gaps with the remaining rice. Form the whole piece into a square log.
3. Lift near and far edges of the mat, and wrap with *nori* by joining both ends of mat, held in your hands.

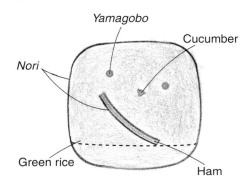

Makes 1 roll
2-2½ cups vinegared rice (p 86)
1 sheet toasted *nori*
Egg *soboro* (p 5)
Cucumber
***Yamagobo* pickles (pokeweed)**
Sliced cooked ham

1. Fold egg *soboro* into the rice to make yellow rice. Peel cucumber lengthwise to make a thin strip.
2. Lay a full sheet of *nori* on a bamboo mat. Mound some of the green rice in the center. Position mouth of cooked ham, nose of *yamagobo*, and eyes of cucumber, filling any gaps with the yellow rice. Form the whole piece into a triangle log.
3. Lift near and far edges of the mat, wrap with *nori* by joining both ends of mat held in your hands, and check the shape.

ANGRY FACE

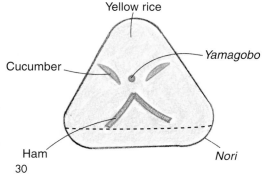

SMILEY FACE

Makes 1 roll
2-2½ cups vinegared rice (p 86)
2 sheet toasted *nori*
Yamagobo **pickles (pokeweed)**
Slice cooked ham
1 Tbsp *katsuobushi* **(dried bonito**
   shavings)
½ Tbsp white sesame seeds
Dash Soy sauce

1. Combine *katsuobushi* and sesame seeds with a dash of soy sauce until just moistened. Combine this with ⅓ of the rice to make brown rice.
2. Lay a full sheet of *nori* on a bamboo mat. Mound some of the white rice in the center of it, from side to side. Position mouth of cooked ham, nose of *yamagobo*, and eyes of thinly cut *nori* strips, by filling any gaps with more white rice. Top with the brown rice, and form the whole piece into a cylinder.
3. Lift near and far edges of the mat, and wrap with *nori* by joining both ends of the mat held in your hands.

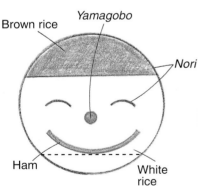

Brown rice
Yamagobo
Nori
Ham
White rice

You can freely arrange the features by changing the curves of mouth and eyes.

SUNSHINE

Makes 1 roll
1½-2 cups vinegared rice (p 86)
1 sheet toasted *nori*
***Tamagoyaki* (thick omelet - p 69)**
2-3 sticks *yamagobo* pickles (pokeweed)

1. Slice off corners of the thick omelet to form a cylinder of 1"(2.5 cm) diameter.
2. Lay a full sheet of *nori* on a bamboo mat. Spread the rice over it. Position 6 thinly cut *yamagobo* sticks at an interval, pressing into the rice.
3. Center the omelet. Lift near and far edges of the mat, and join them in your hands. Overlap the ends of *nori* to secure.

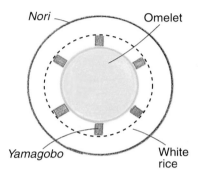

Nori   Omelet
Yamagobo   White rice

Makes 1 roll
2-2½ cups vinegared rice (p 86)
2 sheets toasted *nori*
***Aonori* (green seaweed sprinkles)**
Simmered *kampyo* (p 82)
***Tamagoyaki* (thick omelet - p 69)**
Boiled carrot

1. Fold *aonori* into a quarter portion of the rice. Place some on a 3"(8 cm) strip of *nori*. Positioning thinly cut (⅛"/ 3mm) omelet and boiled carrot sticks, fill any gaps with more green rice to form a well-pressed, triangular log.
2. Make trunk by wrapping layered *kampyo* strips in 3"(8 cm) strip of *nori*.
3. Lay a full sheet of *nori* on a bamboo mat. Spread some white rice over it. Place trank, then stand the triangular log, and add more white rice to hold them in place. Press the whole piece into a cylinder. Join both edges of the mat.

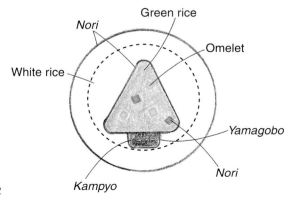

Green rice
Nori
Omelet
White rice
Yamagobo
Nori
Kampyo

CHRISTMAS TREE

HOME SWEET HOME

Makes 1 roll
2-2½ cups vinegared rice (p 86)
2 sheets toasted *nori*
***Yukari* (*shiso* sprinkles)**
Fish sausage or hot dog, cut into sticks

1. Fold *yukari* into ⅙ of the rice to make purple rice.
2. Cut a 3"(8 cm) strip of *nori*, wrap up the purple rice, forming into a triangular log.
3. Make window. Cut the square cut fish sausage into quarters lengthwise (⅜"/1 cm wide and thick) and sandwich thin strips of *nori* to make a crisscross.
4. Place a small amount of white rice on a 3½"(9 cm) strip of *nori*, place window, and roll up. Form into a square log.
5. Lay a full sheet of *nori* on a bamboo mat. Spread the white rice (save some for later) over it. Place the square log in the center, then triangle. Press the remaining rice onto them filling in any gaps, and form a cylinder.
6. Lift near and far edges of the mat, and join them in your hands tightly. Overlap the ends of *nori* to secure.

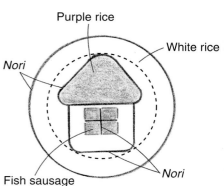

Purple rice

White rice

Nori

Nori

Fish sausage

HOSOMAKI (THIN ROLLS)

Bite-size *hosomaki* rolls are always a favorite at parties. It is best to choose solid fillings such as *tamagoyaki* and hot dog.

SUN

Makes 1 roll
½ cup vinegared rice (p 86)
1 sheet toasted *nori*
***Tobiko* (salted flying fish roe)**
2-3 sticks *yamagobo* pickles (pokeweed)

1. Fold *tobiko* into a quarter portion of the rice to make orange rice.
2. Cut a 4"(10 cm) strip of *nori*, and roll up the yellow rice to make a thin cylinder.
3. Spread the remaining rice over a half sheet of *nori* placed on a bamboo mat. Push 7-8 thinly cut *yamagobo* into the rice at an interval.
4. Center the cylinder and roll up.

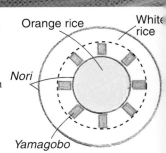

Orange rice · White rice · Nori · Yamagobo

CRESCENT

Makes 1 roll
½ cup vinegared rice (p 86)
1 sheet toasted *nori*
***Tobiko* (salted flying fish roe)**

1. Fold *tobiko* into a quarter portion of the rice to make orange rice.
2. Place the orange rice on a 3"(8 cm) strip of *nori*, and roll into a crescent shape log.
3. Spread some white rice over a half sheet of *nori* placed on a bamboo mat, and center the crescent. Filling any gaps with the remaining rice, form a cylinder. Lift the near edge of the mat, and roll up.

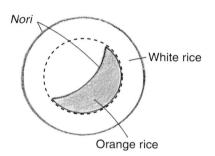

STAR

Makes 1 roll
½ cup vinegared rice (p 86)
½ sheet toasted *nori*
***Tamagoyaki* (thick omelet - p 69)**

1. Remove corners of omelet to make a ¾"(2 cm) cylinder. Make 5 notches into *tamagoyaki* to form a star shape.
2. Spread some white rice over a half sheet of *nori* placed on a bamboo mat, and place the star shaped omelet. Filling any gaps with the remaining rice, form a cylinder. Lift the near edge of the mat, and roll up.

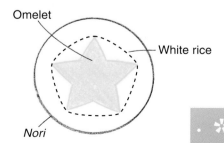

CROSS

Makes 1 roll
½ cup vinegared rice (p 86)
1 sheet toasted *nori*
Simmered *kampyo* (p 82)

1. Cut two 2½"(6 cm) strips of *nori*. Cut *kampyo* into the same lengh as the *nori*, and wrap it in the *nori* strip. Make 2.
2. Spread some white rice over a half sheet of *nori* placed on a bamboo mat. Fold a wrapped *kampyo* strip to form a "V", and place upside down. Add some rice to the sides, and place another "V" shaped *kampyo* strip.
3. Fill any gaps with the remaining rice, forming into a cylinder. Roll up.

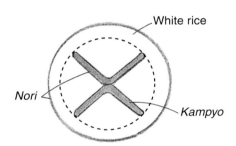

HEART

Makes 1 roll
½ cup vinegared rice (p 86)
1 sheet toasted *nori*
***Sakura dembu* (cod flakes)**

1. Fold *sakura dembu* into ⅓ portion of the rice to make pink rice, and set aside until excess moisture is absorbed.
2. On a ⅓ sheet of *nori*, place pink rice and roll into a heart shape.
3. Spread white rice over a half sheet of *nori*, and center the heart. Add more rice to form a cylinder, and roll up.

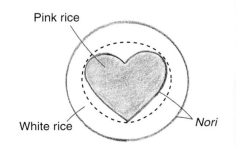

WHIRLPOOL

Makes 1 roll
½ **cup vinegared rice (p 86)**
1 sheet toasted *nori*
Sakura dembu **(cod flakes)**
Egg *soboro* **(p 5)**
Aonori **(green seaweed sprinkles)**

1. Divide the rice into quarter portions. Fold *sakura dembu* into one portion of the rice, and set aside. Fold another portion with egg *soboro*, and another with *aonori*. Save the remaining quarter portion, uncolored.

2. Cut a 5"(13 cm) strip of *nori*, and place on a bamboo mat. Arrange the rice on it, beginning from the near edge: pink, yellow, green and white, ending with less grains of rice.

3. Lift near edge of the mat, press the edge into the pink or yellow rice, and roll up.

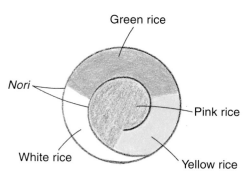

Green rice

Nori

White rice

Pink rice

Yellow rice

MORE HANA SUSHI PATTERNS

If you get used to making Hana Sushi, challenge yourself to create your own rolls for such occasions as anniversaries or birthdays. Here are several hints to please your recipients. Refer to page 5 for coloring suggestions.

FOUR-LEAF CLOVER

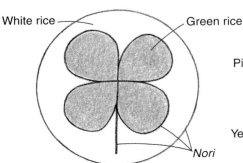

White rice — Green rice — Nori

1. Make a teardrop shape by folding in green rice with *nori*. Repeat to make 4.
2. Assemble leaves and a stem of *nori*, and fill any gaps with the white rice. Spread white rice over *nori*, put the leaves in the center, and roll up.

RAINBOW

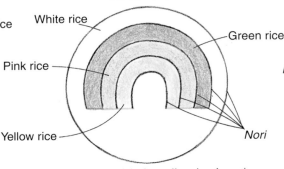

White rice — Green rice — Pink rice — Yellow rice — Nori

1. Layer green, pink, then yellow rice alternating with *nori*. Roll into an oval, and cut into halves.
2. Spread white rice over *nori*, place rainbow, and roll up, filling the gaps with more of the rice.

LEMON SLICE

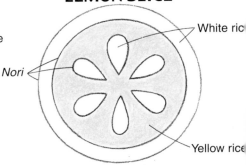

White ric — Nori — Yellow rice

1. Make 6 small teardrops with white rice and *nori*.
2. Filling in the gaps, position each in yellow rice, and roll up. Roll again with white rice.

WATERMELON

White rice — Red rice — Green rice — Nori — Black sesame seeds (Place on each slice)

1. Make a small red rice roll. Spread green rice on *nori*, place the red roll, and roll up. Cut into halves, and cover the cut edge with *nori*.
2. Roll in white rice. Position black sesame seeds after slicing.

BALLOON

Yellow rice — Rice — Nori — Black sesame seeds (Place on each slice) — Omelet

1. Make a roll of yellow rice.
2. Set the balloon and thick omelet strip cut into triangular log, plus a strip of *nori* for the string by pressing with white rice. Roll up.

FUNNY FROG

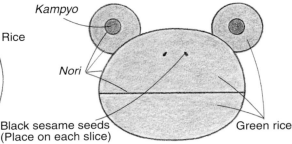

Kampyo — Nori — Black sesame seeds — Green rice

1. Make a green rice roll. Cut into halves and cover the cut edge with *nori* to make mouth. Assemble the halves again, and wrap in another sheet of *nori*.
2. Make ears with green rice and *nori*-wrapped *kampyo* strips. Slice off to form a dome shape, and stick to the head. Position nostrils of black sesame seeds after slicing.

PAPER DOLL

Black sesame seeds (Place on each slice) — White rice — White rice — Nori

1. Make a thin roll of white rice. Make a triangle log for body, and slice off its tip. Stick to the head.
2. Roll with white rice and *nori*. Position eyes of black sesame seeds after slicing.

TRAFFIC LIGHTS

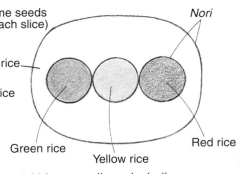

Nori — White rice — Green rice — Yellow rice — Red rice

1. Make green, yellow and red rolls.
2. Spread white rice over *nori*, position the three in a row, and roll up, filling in the gaps, into an oval shape.

RAINY DAY

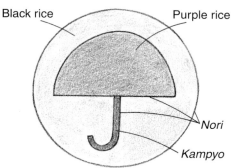

Black rice · Purple rice · Nori · Kampyo

1. Make a roll of purple rice, and cut into halves lengthwise. Cover the cut edge with *nori*. Make handle by wrapping *nori* around *kampyo* strips.
2. Assemble them into an umbrella, and roll up with black rice.

MT. FUJI

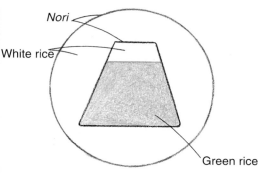

Nori · White rice · Green rice

1. Place green rice on *nori*, top with white rice. Roll up and form a trapezoid.
2. Roll up again with white rice and *nori*.

GERBERA DAISY

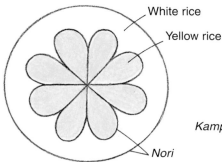

White rice · Yellow rice · Nori

1. Make 8 teardrops with yellow rice and *nori*.
2. Assemble them into a flower, and roll up with white rice and *nori*.

ALPHABET

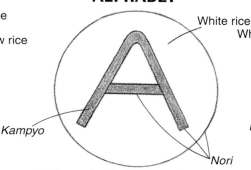

White rice · Kampyo · Nori

1. Wrap any length of *kampyo* strips with *nori*.
2. Form a letter as you fill any gaps with white rice, and roll up.

FISH

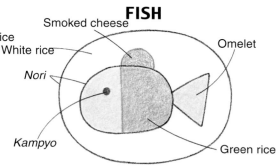

Smoked cheese · White rice · Omelet · Nori · Kampyo · Green rice

1. Make a thin roll of yellow rice, including a *kampyo* strip; cut into halves. Make another roll of green rice, and cut off an edge. Join them by sticking the cut edges together. Roll up in *nori*.
2. Cut thick omelet into triangular sticks. Cut smoked cheese into halves. Assemble body and fins by adding some white rice around them, and roll up.

CHICKABIDDY

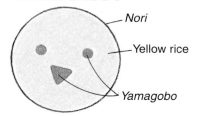

Nori · Yellow rice · Yamagobo

Form a very thin cylinder of yellow rice, and set *yamagobo* sticks into it. Roll up with some more yellow rice and *nori*.

ANNIVERSARY RING

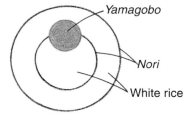

Yamagobo · Nori · White rice

1. Make a very thin roll with white rice. Make a slit into it, and insert a *yamagobo* root.
2. Roll up in more rice and *nori*.

QUARTET

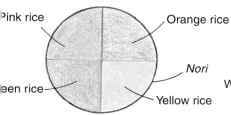

Pink rice · Orange rice · Nori · Green rice · Yellow rice

1. Roll a very thin roll of each color. Cut each roll into quarters lengthwise.
2. Join the quarters, and roll up with *nori*.

BLOOMING FLOWER

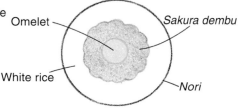

Omelet · Sakura dembu · White rice · Nori

Spread white rice over *nori*, spread *sakura dembu* in the center, then place rounded thick omelet. Roll up.

SUSHI BENTO

Sushi rolled with a flower motif enhances any kind of dish. These tasty morsels combining rich, salty and sweet flavors will enhance the lovely Hana Sushi in any picnic lunch, not to mention *hanami*, or cherry blossom viewing.

Simmered Sweet Potato

1 sweet potato
1½ cups water
2 Tbsps sugar

1. Slice sweet potato into ⅜"(1 cm) rounds, and soak in water for 5 minutes.
2. Put drained sweet potato slices in a small saucepan, and cook with water and sugar over low heat until soft.

Sausage Rolls

4 cocktail wieners
4 strips of bacon
Vegetable oil

1. Cut wieners and bacon into halves. Wrap bacon around wiener, and secure ends with a wooden pick.
2. Heat oil in a frying pan, and cook wiener rolls until heated through.

Soboro Pumpkin

¼ Japanese pumpkin
3 oz (90 g) ground chicken
2 cups *dashi* stock
3 Tbsps soy sauce
1 Tbsp *mirin*
2 tsps sugar

1. Peel pumpkin, and cut into bite-size pieces.
2. Heat *dashi*, soy sauce, *mirin* and sugar in a saucepan. Add pumpkin and ground chicken. Cook until the pumpkin is soft.

Sesame Tuna

1 fillet fresh tuna
White sesame seeds (raw)
2 Tbsps soy sauce
1 Tbsp *mirin*
Cornstarch for dusting
Vegetable oil

1. Slice tuna into 1"(2.5 cm) thickness, and marinate in soy sauce and *mirin* mixture for 20 minutes or longer. Drain and dust with cornstarch. Toss with sesame seeds until completely covered.
2. Heat ample oil in a frying pan, and fry both sides until golden.

Shrimp and Broad Bean Tempura

7 oz (200 g) shelled shrimp
4 oz (120 g) shelled young broad beans
Tempura Batter:
  1 cup all-purpose flour
  1 cup ice water
  1 egg, beaten
Oil for deep-frying

1. Devein shrimp. Boil beans only briefly; drain.
2. Combine *tempura* batter ingredients lightly, and add shrimp and beans. Take a bite-size portion of the mixture on a spatula, and slide into heated oil. Fry until crisp and golden over moderate heat.

Fried Wonton

3 oz (90 g) ground pork
2 Tbsps minced *negi* (long onion)
  Salt and pepper
  ½ tsp soy sauce
  1 tsp cornstarch
1 dozen wonton wrappers
Oil for deep-frying

1. Mix ground pork and *negi*, stirring until smooth and sticky. Stir in salt, pepper, soy sauce and cornstarch.
2. Divide the mixture into 12, and wrap each portion in a wonton wrapper. Deep-fry until crisp and lightly browned.

Sauteed Prawns

8 prawns
  Salt and pepper
Oil for frying
Lemon wedge

1. Shell and devein prawns. Slit each along the back and open flat.
2. Heat oil in a frying pan, and saute prawns just until done. Sprinkle salt and pepper. Add a wedge of lemon to serve.

Simmered Konnyaku and Fishcake

1 cake *konnyaku* (yam jelly)
1 package fried fishcake (*Satsuma-age*)
½ pod dried chili pepper, sliced
½ cup *dashi* stock
1 Tbsp each soy sauce and *mirin*
½ tsp sugar

1. Score surface of *konnyaku* in a lattice pattern, on both sides. This makes the seasonings seep in. Cut into 1"(2.5 cm) cubes. Remove excess oil from fried fishcake by pouring boiling water over. Cut into bite-size pieces.
2. Heat *dashi*, soy sauce, *mirin* and sugar in a saucepan, and add *konnyaku* and fishcake. Simmer over low heat until the liquid is gone.

SUSHI BENTO

To aviod spoilage during the warmer seasons, be sure to carry well-cooked, deeply seasoned foods to accompany Hana Sushi. This is an example for family summer outings.

Curried Calamari

1 squid, skinned
  Salt and pepper
  All-purpose flour, mixed with
    Curry powder
Vegetable oil for frying

1. Score squid in a lattice pattern. Cut into bite-size pieces and sprinkle with salt and pepper. Dust with curry powder and flour mixture.
2. Heat oil in a frying pan, and saute both sides.

Ginger Scallops

1 dozen steamed scallops
1 small piece fresh ginger
⅓ cup rice wine
¼ cup soy sauce

1. Shred ginger.
2. Heat rice wine in a saucepan, and heat until the alcohol evaporates. Add scallops, ginger and soy sauce, and simmer until the sauce is absorbed.

Sauteed Sausages

4 cocktail wieners
Oil for frying

1. Make scores on one side of each wiener.
2. Cut into bite-size pieces, and saute in heated oil until the outside is crisp.

Sweet Potato Tempura

½ lb (220 g) sweet potato
Tempura **Batter**
   ⅔ cup all-purpose flour
   ⅔ cup ice water
   1 egg, beaten
Oil for deep-frying
Toasted *nori*

1. Cut sweet potato into 2"(5 cm) long sticks, and soak in water for 5 minutes; drain and wipe off moisture.
2 Combine the ingredients for *tempura* batter only lightly (do not stir vigorously). Dip sweet potato sticks in the batter, and deep-fry one by one over moderate heat. Drain oil, cool, and wrap a strip of *nori* around each.

Salmon Teriyaki

2 fillets fresh salmon
1 Tbsp soy sauce
1 Tbsp *mirin*
Vegetable oil for frying

1. Cut salmon into bite-size pieces.
2. Heat vegetable oil in a frying pan, and cook salmon pieces just until heated through. Reduce heat, add soy sauce and *mirin*, and stir until the salmon is coated with the thickened sauce.

4 *chikuwa* **(grilled fishcake) rolls**
8 *shiso* **leaves**
Tempura **Batter**
   ⅔ cup all-purpose flour
   ⅔ cup ice water
   1 egg, beaten
Oil for deep-frying

Fishcake Tempura

1. Cut *chikuwa* rolls into halves, and wrap a *shiso* leaf around each.
2. Combine the ingredients for *tempura* batter lightly (do not stir vigorously). Dip *shiso*-wrapped *chikuwa* in the batter, and deep-fry over moderate heat until the outside is crisp.

Spicy Fried Fish

2 fillets any white meat fish
Salt and pepper
All-purpose flour for dusting
Curry powder
Oil for deep-frying

1. Cut fish into bite-size pieces, and sprinkle with salt and pepper.
2. Mix 2 part flour with one part curry powder, and coat fish pieces in a plastic bag. Deep-fry over moderate heat until golden.

Paprika Flowers

1 green bell pepper
4 quail eggs
Salt and pepper
Oil for frying

1. Slice bell pepper into ⅜"(1 cm) rings.
2. Heat oil in a frying pan, and place pepper rings. Break a quail egg into each ring, and cook until done. Sprinkle with salt and pepper.

Veggie Spring Rolls

2 oz (60 g) string beans
1 medium carrot
1 fish sausage
3 spring roll wrappers, quartered
1 Tbsp cornstarch, dissolved in 1 Tbsp water
Oil for deep-frying

1. Blanch string beans and cut into 1½"(4 cm) pieces. Cut carrots and sausage into sticks of the same length.
2. Roll up vegetables and fish sausage sticks in a wrapper, and seal the edge using the cornstarch/water mixture. Deep-fry until golden, and drain oil.

Braised Lotus Root and Chicken

1 small lotus root (5 oz/150 g)
5 oz (150 g) boneless chicken thigh
1 Tbsp each, soy sauce and *mirin*
1½ Tbsps sesame oil for frying

1. Cut lotus root into rolling wedges or bite-size pieces, and soak in vinegared water for 10 minutes. Cut chicken into bite-size pieces.
2. Heat the sesame oil in a frying pan, and stir-fry chicken and drained lotus root over high heat. When they are heated through, swirl in soy sauce and *mirin*. Keep stirring, until the sauce is almost reduced.

SUSHI BENTO

These crisp-fried tidbits match the refreshing, light taste of sushi. Use any seasonal ingredients, so long as they do not get soggy after a while.

7 oz (200 g) chicken thigh, cut up
   2 Tbsps soy sauce
   1 Tbsp *mirin*
   1 clove garlic, grated
2 Tbsps cornstarch
Oil for deep-frying

1. Marinate chicken pieces in soy sauce, *mirin* and garlic mixture for about 20 minutes.
2. Pat dry chicken pieces, and toss in cornstarch until thoroughly coated. Deep-fry over moderate heat until lightly browned.

Fried Chicken

Boiled Prawns

8 prawns, shelled and deveined
Salt to taste
Dash white wine

Bring water to a boil, add white wine and salt, and boil prawns just until done. Do not overcook.

Originated not in Japan but in California, these sushi rolls feature salad-like fillings, and their popularity has grown at an explosive pace thanks to their healthy combination of ingredients.

YAKINIKU (KOREAN BARBECUE) ROLL

Makes 1 roll
1½ cups vinegared rice (p 86)
1 sheet toasted *nori*
Toasted white sesame seeds
Several okra pods, blanched
***Mizuna* greens**
2 oz (60 g) beef sirloin, thinly sliced
½ Tbsp *teriyaki* **sauce**
Vegetable oil for frying

1. Coat a heated frying pan with oil. Cook beef slices in it briefly, and swirl in *teriyaki* sauce. When the liquid is reduced, remove from heat and let cool.
2. Place the *nori* sheet over a plastic wrap cut larger than the *nori*. Spread the rice all over it. Sprinkle evenly with sesame seeds. Press the surface gently lest the sesame seeds should fall off when turned over.
3. Turn over gently, using both hands. Place beef, okura and *mizuna* greens, and roll up. Wrap in the plastic wrap, and press gently using a bamboo mat.

Hints for Variations:
Feel free to try a brand-new combination using the same technique.

Substitute fillings with:
Tuna + scallion + mayonnaise
Pork cutlet + shredded cabbage
Teriyaki chicken + green leaf lettuce, etc.

Substitute white sesame seeds with:
Black sesame seeds
Tobiko (salted flying fish roe)
Aonori (green seaweed sprinkles)
Shredded *shiso* leaves
Yukari (*shiso* sprinkles)
Salmon flakes, etc.

HOW TO ROLL URAMAKI (INSIDE-OUT ROLLS)

Makes 1 roll
1½ cups vinegared rice (p 86)
1 sheet toasted *nori*
Salmon *sashimi*, cut into sticks
Avocado slices, sprinkled
   with lemon juice
2-3 Tbsps toasted sesame seeds
Scallions
Green leaf lettuce

1 Place the *nori* over plastic wrap to prevent sticking. Spread the rice over it, from edge to edge. Sprinkle with generous amount of sesame seeds all over.

2 Using your palms, press the sesame seeds gently to prevent them from falling off.

3 Lift the edge gently, and turn over, so as not to let the rice or sesame seeds fall apart.

4 Place lettuce, salmon, avocado and scallions, and lift the near edge to start rolling.

5 Roll up and wrap with the plastic wrap.

6 Roll and shape with a bamboo mat. Tighten the roll by pressing the mat.

Rolling Up with Mat

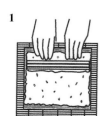

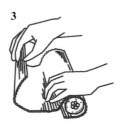

1. Lay a bamboo rolling mat, flat side up. Place a sheet of *nori* over it, aligning the near edges. Spread rice all over it, and arrange the fillings.
2. Lift the near end of the mat, and press against the fillings. Lift the edge of the mat slightly, and roll up.
3. Hold the roll with both of your hands, pressing carefully but tightly. Press both ends to flatten. Let stand, with the end of *nori* facing down, until the roll is securely sealed.

HAM AND EGG SALAD ROLL

Makes 1 roll
1½ cups vinegared rice (p 86)
1 sheet toasted *nori*
2 Tbsps *tobiko* (salted flying fish roe)
2 slices cooked ham
***Mizuna* greens**
Green leaf lettuce
½ hard boiled egg, chopped
½ Tbsp mayonnaise
1 tsp minced pickles
Salt and pepper

1. Combine boiled egg, mayonnaise, pickles, salt and pepper.
2. Place the *nori* over a plastic wrap, and spread the rice over it from edge to edge. Sprinkle *tobiko* all over. Press gently to keep the rice and *tobiko* in place.
3. Turn over gently. Place ham, egg mixture, *mizuna* and lettuce. Roll up, wrap in the plastic wrap, and tighten the roll with a bamboo mat.

PRAWN SALAD ROLL

Makes 1 roll
1½ cups vinegared rice (p 86)
1 sheet toasted *nori*
2 prawns, boiled
***Aonori* (green seaweed sprinkles)**
Green leaf lettuce
3-4 stalks green asparagus, cooked
Chives

1. Place the *nori* over a plastic wrap. Spread the rice over it from edge to edge. Sprinkle with *aonori*, and press down gently.
2. Turn over carefully. Place prawns, lettuce, asparagus and chives; roll up.

AVOCADO TUNA ROLL

Make neat stripes with thin avocado slices. Tuna *sashimi* and avocado makes one of the best combinations for sushi. Serve with *wasabi*.

Makes 1 roll
1½ cups vinegared rice (p 86)
1 avocado, stoned and peeled
2 oz(60 g) tuna *sashimi*, cut into
  ⅜"(1 cm) wide strips
Lemon juice
***Wasabi* paste**

1. Lay a plastic wrap. Slice avocado thinly, and arrange on the plastic wrap. Sprinkle with lemon juice.
2. Spread the rice over the avocado slices. Place *sashimi* strips, and roll up.

SMOKED SALMON ROLL

Shiso compliments smoked salmon, while cucumber provides crunchiness.

Makes 1 roll
1½ cups vinegared rice (p 86)
3 oz(90 g) smoked salmon, sliced
Cucumber, shredded
***Shiso* leaves**

1. Lay a plastic wrap. Arrange smoked salmon slices over it. Spread the rice over them from edge to edge.
2. Place *shiso* leaves and shredded cucumber, and roll up.

TROPICAL ROLL

A harmony of pineapple and luncheon meat, wrapped in vinegared rice and accompanied by refreshing veggies.

Makes 1 roll
1½ cups vinegared rice (p 86)
1 sheet toasted *nori*
Canned luncheon meat
Canned pineapples
Green leaf lettuce
Red bell pepper
Chives

1. Place the *nori* on a bamboo mat, and spread the rice all over, leaving the far edge of the *nori* uncovered.
2. Cut luncheon meat and bell pepper into ⅜"(1 cm) thick julienne strips. Cut well-drained pineapples into small pieces. Place all the fillings in a line from side to side. Lift the near edge of the mat, and press it into the fillings to pack everything tightly. Roll up and let stand, edge down, until securely sealed.

CHICKEN TERIYAKI ROLL

Richly seasoned chicken filling combined with asparagus and crunchy *enoki* mushrooms.

Makes 1 roll
1½ cups vinegared rice (p 86)
1 sheet toasted *nori*
***Teriyaki* chicken (see below)**
***Enoki* mushrooms**
Green asparagus, cooked
Green leaf lettuce

Teriyaki Chicken
3½ oz (100 g) chicken thigh, cut up
1 Tbsp soy sauce
1 Tbsp *mirin*
Vegetable oil for frying

1. Heat vegetable oil in a frying pan, and cook chicken just until heated through. Reduce heat, add soy sauce and *mirin*, and stir until coated with the thickened sauce. Cut into ⅜"(1 cm) wide sticks.
2. Place the *nori* on a bamboo mat. Spread the rice over the *nori*, leaving the far edge of the *nori* uncovered.
3. Place all the fillings in a line from side to side. Lift the near edge of the mat, press it down into the fillings to pack everything in place, and roll up. Let stand, edge down, until securely sealed.

ALASKAN ROLL

The golden trio of salmon, avocado and scallion. Add a lemon zest to serve.

Makes 1 roll
1½ cups vinegared rice (p 86)
1 sheet toasted *nori*
Salmon *sashimi*
Avocado, cut into sticks
Scallions
Lemon

1. Sprinkle avocado sticks with lemon juice to prevent discoloring.
2. Place the *nori* on a bamboo mat, and spread the rice over it (leave the far edge of the *nori* uncovered).
3. Cut the salmon into sticks, and place on the rice in a line from side to side. Add the avocado and scallion. Lift the near edge of the mat, and press it into the fillings to pack everything tightly, and roll up. Let stand, the edge of the *nori* down, until secured.
4. Serve with a slice of lemon.

Instant Tororo Soup

½ cup *Tororo kombu* (kelp shavings)
4 cups boiling water
***Mitsuba* (trefoil)**
4 tsps soy sauce
Few drops sesame oil

Put *tororo* in a serving bowl, and pour boiling water over it. Stir in the salt and soy sauce, and garnish with *mitsuba* (trefoil).

Fisherman's Soup

16 clams
4 cups water
Scallions, chopped
1 tsp sea salt
Few drops soy sauce

In a saucepan, heat clams and water to a boil. When the shells are opened, add the salt and soy sauce, and remove from heat. Serve sprinkled with chopped scallions.

Egg Drop Soup

2 eggs, beaten well
2 lettuce leaves, shredded
½ red bell pepper, diced
4 cups *dashi* stock
1 tsp salt
Few drops soy sauce

Heat the *dashi* stock, salt and soy sauce to a boil, and drizzle the beaten eggs slowly, stirring constantly over low heat. When the egg floats, add lettuce and pepper, and remove from heat. Do not overcook since the fluffy texture of the egg will be spoiled.

Rice Vermicelli and Beef Soup

⅔ oz (20 g) rice vermicelli
4 oz (120 g) beef loin, thinly sliced
Scallions, cut into 1"(2.5 cm)
Toasted white sesame seeds
4 cups *dashi* or chicken stock
2 tsps soy sauce
Dash of white pepper

1. Soak rice vermicelli in boiling water until supple; drain and cut up. Cut beef slices into bite size.
2. Heat the stock to a boil, and add vermicelli and beef. Sprinkle with pepper. Serve hot, garnished with scallions and sesame seeds.

Onsen Egg Miso Soup

4 eggs
4 sprigs watercress
4 cups *dashi* stock
4 Tbsps *miso* (soybean paste)

1. Break one egg each into 4 small, ovenproof dishes. Pour 1 Tbsp water (extra) on top of each egg. Do not stir. Microwave 4 dishes together for about 1 minute 30 seconds in a 600W electronic range. Transfer soft-boiled eggs into each serving bowl.
2. Heat the *dashi* stock to a boil, stir in the *miso*, and return to a boil. Pour into serving bowls and top each with a sprig of watercress.

Wakame and Okra Soup

⅙ oz(5 g) dried *wakame*
6 okra pods, thinly sliced
4 cups *dashi* or chicken stock

1. Soak dried *wakame* in water at least 5 minutes until softened; cut up.
2. Heat the stock to a boil, and cook *wakame* and okra just until heated. (*Wakame* seaweed can be eaten without cooking. Too much cooking may cause discoloring.)

Pickled Myoga Sprouts

6-8 fresh *myoga* sprouts
1 cup sushi vinegar

Split *myoga* lengthwise in half, and soak in the sushi vinegar. Marinate for 2 hours or until supple in refrigerator.

Komatsuna Greens in Mustard Dressing

½ bunch *komatsuna* greens, cooked and cut up
3 Tbsps *jako* (semi-dried or dried baby sardines)
1 Tbsp soy sauce
1 tsp *mirin*
½ tsp Japanese hot mustard paste

Combine the soy sauce, *mirin* and mustard to make dressing. Toss *komatsuna* greens and sardines in it, until evenly coated.

Pickled Peppers

½ each, red, orange and yellow bell peppers
1 cup sushi vinegar

Seed bell peppers, and cut into ⅜"(1 cm) wide strips. Soak in sushi vinegar overnight in refrigerator.

Okras in Sesame Dressing

1 dozen okra pods
2 Tbsps black sesame seeds, freshly ground
1 Tbsp rice wine
2 tsps sugar
2 tsps soy sauce

1. Blanch okras in boiling water briefly, and cut diagonally into bite-size pieces.
2. Combine ground sesame seeds, rice wine, sugar and soy sauce. Toss okra in this sauce until evenly coated.

Radish in Yuzu Pepper Dressing

¼ medium *daikon*
1 tsp *yuzu kosho* (*yuzu* and green chili paste)
1 tsp salt
Young *daikon* leaves, cut up

1. Peel *daikon*, and cut into rolling wedges (Cut lengthwise into quarters, and then cut into chunks diagonally, turning the *daikon* after each cut. This way, the vegetable can absorb flavors quickly, maintaining some of the crispness.) In a bowl, sprinkle *daikon* pieces with the salt, and rub them as if kneading bread dough, until supple.
2 Squeeze *daikon* to remove extra moisture and salt. Toss with the *yuzu kosho* until evenly coated. Serve garnished with *daikon* greens.

Lotus Root and Tarako Salad

3½ oz(100 g) fresh lotus root
2 oz (60 g) or 1 small *tarako* (salted cod roe)

1. Peel and cut lotus root lengthwise into quarters. Slice thinly, and soak in vinegared water for about 10 minutes to prevent discoloring. Cook in boiling vinegared water only for a minute; drain.
2. Skin the *tarako*, and mix well with the mayonnaise. Stir in lotus root slices until evenly coated.

SUSHI CANAPES

Requiring no equipment or techniques to prepare, these colorful combinations are perfect for those who don't care to use a rolling mat. Shown here is a variation of *gunkan* style *nigiri* sushi(*gunkan maki*), topped with flowers made of delicacies.

EGG FLOWER

Arrange boiled quail egg slices into tiny petals, and center with *ikura*.

Makes 1
¼ cup vinegared *rice* (p 86)
One 1" (2.5 cm - ⅛ sheet) strip toasted *nori*
1 quail egg, boiled and sliced
1 heap tsp *ikura* (salted salmon roe)

1. Take the rice in your hand, and press to shape a short cylinder. Wrap the *nori* around it, but do not trim off excess *nori*.
2. Arrange boiled quail egg slices in a flower shape, and top with a mound of *ikura*.

TAKANA FLOWER

Crunchy *yamagobo* petals surround the center, filled with flavorful *takana* pickles.

Makes 1
¼ cup vinegared rice (p 86)
One 1" (2.5 cm - ⅛ sheet) strip toasted *nori*
Yamagobo pickles (pokeweed), sliced
Takana (mustard) green pickles, chopped
Thin omelet (p 69), shredded

1. Take the rice in your hand, and press into a short cylinder, using both hands. Wrap the *nori* around it, but do not trim off excess *nori*, as it will shrink in time.
2. Arrange *yamagobo* petals, and top with chopped *takana* pickles. Arrange shredded omelet on the center.

SHRIMP FLOWER

Press the center of the rice to make indentation, lest the toppings should fall off.

Makes 1
¼ cup vinegared rice (p 86)
One 1" (2.5 cm - ⅛ sheet) strip toasted *nori*
5 shrimp, boiled in salty water
1 heap tsp *tobiko* (salted flying fish roe)

1. Take the rice in your hand, and press into a short cylinder, using both hands. Wrap the *nori* around it, but do not trim off excess *nori*.
2. Arrange shrimp to form petals, and center a mound of *tobiko*.

SALMON FLOWER

Lovely floret of pink salmon and yellow. The leaves are made of pea pods.

Makes 1
¼ cup vinegared rice (p 86)
Thin omelet (p 69), cut into 1" (2.5 cm) strip
***Mitsuba* (trefoil) stalk, briefly boiled**
2-3 slices smoked salmon
Egg *soboro* (p 5)
Pea pod, briefly boiled

1. Take the rice in your hand, and press into a short cylinder, using both hands. Wrap the thin omelet around it, and secure it by tying with supple *mitsuba* stalk.
2. Arrange smoked salmon slices (cut if necessary) into a flower, and place egg *soboro* in its center. Cut a cooked pea pod diagonally into halves, and insert them from a side.

MAKING GUNKAN MAKI

The *gunkan maki* style base can hold loose ingredients such as *ikura*, *tobiko*, or sea urchin. Wet your fingers with vinegared water. Just like making a *nigiri* sushi finger, press a morsel of vinegared rice into an oval or ball. Wrap it with a *nori* strip that is cut a little higher than the rice finger to make a "cup." If wrapping in a strip of thin omelet, bind it with *mitsuba* (trefoil) or simmered *kampyo* (gourd strip) since the omelet does not stick to rice naturally.

Toasted *nori* sheet shrinks when it absorbs the moisture of rice. To avoid breakage of *nori*, use a longer strip than needed.

DECORATIVE CUTTING

It's easier than you think! With just a slice of *kamaboko*, or fishcake, an ordinary sushi looks so special. Just follow the drawings.

Makes 1
¼ cup vinegared rice (p 86)
One 1" (2.5 cm - ⅛ sheet) strip toasted *nori*
½ oz(15 g) salmon *sashimi*, chopped
***Shiso* leaf**
Thin slice of pink *kamaboko* (fishcake)

1. Using a paring knife, make slits and holes into *kamaboko* according to the drawing. Make curls referring to the photo.
2. Press the rice into a finger form, and wrap *nori* around its sides. Fill the cup with chopped salmon and *shiso* leaf. Top with the decorative slice of *kamaboko*.

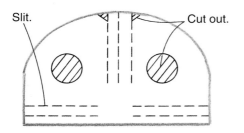

BUTTERFLY

Choose *kamaboko* with pink surface for celebration dinner.

COQUE

Enhance a festive sushi dinner with such an ornamental *gunkan maki*.

Makes 1
¼ cup vinegared rice (p 86)
One 1" (2.5 cm - ⅛ sheet) strip toasted *nori*
1 Tbsp *ikura*
3 cucumber slices
Thin slice of pink *kamaboko* (fishcake)

1. Using a paring knife, make slits and cuts in *kamaboko* according to the drawing. Bring down both sides and make curls.
2. Make a *gunkan maki* with *ikura*, and top with *kamaboko*.

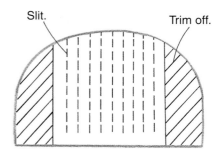

Makes 1
¼ cup vinegared rice (p 86)
One 1" (2.5 cm - ⅛ sheet) strip toasted *nori*
½ oz(15 g) calamari *sashimi*, cut thinly
***Shiso* leaf**
Toasted white sesame seeds
Toasted black sesame seed
Thin slice of pink *kamaboko* (fishcake)

1. Using a paring knife, make slits and cuts in *kamaboko* according to the drawing. Bring down both sides and make curls referring to the photo.
2. Press the rice into a finger form, and wrap *nori* around its sides. Fill the cup with calamari *sashimi*, white sesame seeds, and cover with a *shiso* leaf. Top with a swan shaped *kamaboko*, and place a black sesame seed to mark eye.

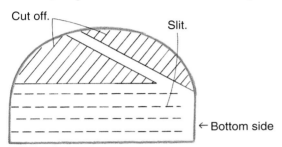

SWAN
Surprise your guests and pique their interest with this intricate-and edible-handiwork.

CRANE
Widely spread wings of the crane backed with *tobiko* and chive toppings.

Makes 1
¼ cup vinegared rice (p 86)
One 1" (2.5 cm - ⅛ sheet) strip toasted *nori*
1 Tbsp *tobiko* (salted flying fish roe)
Chives
Thin slice of pink *kamaboko* (fishcake)
Toasted black sesame seed

1. Using a paring knife, make slits and cuts in *kamaboko* according to the drawing. Pull sides down slightly, and bring the bottom strip towards right to make neck. Make curls.
2. Press the rice into a finger form, and wrap *nori* around its sides. Fill the cup with *tobiko* and chives. Place the crane carefully, and mark eye with a black sesame seed.

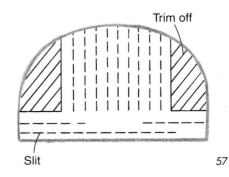

PORCUPINE

A humorous look of porcupine is made of *yukari* rice, carrot thorns and *kamaboko* eyes.

Makes 1
¼ cup vinegared rice (p 86)
One 1" (2.5 cm - ⅛ sheet) strip toasted *nori*
***Yukari* (*shiso* sprinkles)**
***Kamaboko* (fishcake)**
Boiled carrot

1. Toss the rice with *yukari* to make purple rice.
2. Shape the purple rice into an oval, leaving the top fluffy. Wrap the strip of *nori* around the rice.
3. Cut carrot into tapered matchsticks, and insert them into the rice. Make eyes with *kamaboko*, and mark eyes with tiny cuts of *nori*.

LADYBUG

Children will be excited to look at such an adorable little ladybug on their plates.

Makes 1
¼ cup vinegared rice (p 86)
One 1" (2.5 cm - ⅛ sheet) strip toasted *nori*
***Sakura dembu* (cod flakes)**
***Kamaboko* (fishcake)**
Simmered *kampyo* (p 82)

1. Toss the rice with *sakura dembu* to make pink rice, and set aside until excess moisture is absorbed.
2. Shape the rice into an oval mound, and wrap *nori* strip around it.
3. Make eyes with *kamaboko*, spots with *nori*, and lines with *kampyo*, and position carefully.

GOLDFISH

The yellow fish has omelet body and scales. The red fish is made of *sakura dembu*.

Makes 1 each
¼ cup vinegared rice (p 86)
One 1" (2.5 cm - ⅛ sheet) strip toasted *nori*
Pea pod, cooked, or Cucumber peel
Kamaboko (fishcake)

Thin omelet (p 69)
Cooked carrot
1 Tbsp *sakura dembu* (cod flakes)

1. Form the rice into a fish shape, and wrap the *nori* strip around it.
2. Make toppings: For the yellow fish, cut out the fish shape from thin omelet, and place on the rice. Cut out dots from the omelet, and place on the fish.
For the pink fish, spread *sakura dembu* evenly. Make eyes with *kamaboko* and *nori*. Cut out other details from carrot, pea pod and/or cucumber peel. Position them as shown.

For entertainment and parties, a colorful platter of *temari* sushi will show how much you care about your guests. It's so easy once you get used to shape a small rice ball.

CHAKIN TEMARI SUSHI

The thin egg-crepe wrapper, inspired by *chakin*, a small linen used in Tea Ceremony, wraps a rice ball with shrimp inside.

SALMON TEMARI SUSHI

A slice of smoked salmon resembles a tiny camellia blossom with shredded omelet center.

SESAME SEED TEMARI SUSHI

A carrot floret accents this aromatic and crunchy sushi ball. Make the flower as small as possible.

SESAME SEED TEMARI SUSHI

Makes 1
¼ cup vinegared rice (p 86)
1 Tbsp toasted white sesame seeds
Thin omelet (p 69)
Shiso **leaf**
Cooked carrot
Mitsuba **(trefoil), cooked**

1. In a plastic wrap, hold and press the rice into a ball shape.
2. Remove the wrap, and roll in toasted sesame seeds until evenly coated.
3. Trim *shiso* leaf into a tiny leaf shape. Cut thin omelet and carrot into petals. Make center with *mitsuba*. Arrange them on top of the rice ball.

SALMON TEMARI SUSHI

Makes 1
¼ cup vinegared rice (p 86)
1 slice smoked salmon
Thin omelet (p 69), shredded

1. In a plastic wrap, hold and press the rice into a ball shape.
2. Open the wrap, and place a round-cut slice of smoked salmon, and wrap up again. Squeezing the gathered edges of the plastic wrap, press the salmon onto the rice.
3. Remove the wrap. Using a chopstick, make 5 indentations to resemble a flower. Stand a bunch of shredded omelet in the center to resemble a camellia center.

CHAKIN TEMARI SUSHI

Makes 1
¼ cup vinegared rice (p 86)
1-2 shrimp, cooked
Thin omelet (p 69)
Sakura dembu **(cod flakes)**
Cooked ham
Cucumber peel

1. Spread a plastic wrap on your hand, place the rice, centering a shrimp, and wrap up. Press into a ball shape.
2. Remove the wrap. Wrap the ball in the omelet sheet, and then wrap again in the plastic wrap. Squeezing the gathered edges of the wrap, press the omelet to stick to the rice.
3. Remove the wrap. Make a flower with *sakura dembu* on the top, and add a tiny dot of ham and finely cut cucumber peel.

PERSIMMON TEMARI SUSHI

Makes 1
¼ cup vinegared rice (p 86)
Pickled greens, chopped (such as *mibuna* or *nozawana*)
Salmon *sashimi*, chopped
Toasted *nori*

1. Toss the vinegared rice with the pickled greens until evenly mixed.
2. Wrap in a plastic wrap, and press into a ball.
3. Remove the wrap, and top with slitted, square-cut *nori* and salmon *sashimi*.

BOUNCING TEMARI SUSHI

Makes 1
¼ cup vinegared rice (p 86)
***Tobiko* (salted flying fish roe)**
Thin omelet (p 69)
Toasted *nori*, cut into very thin strips
***Shiso* leaves**

1. Toss the vinegared rice with *tobiko* to make orange rice.
2. Wrap in a plastic wrap, and shape into a tiny ball.
3. Remove the wrap, and attach details: lines with *nori* strips, petals with cut-out omelet, and center with *tobiko*. Cut out tiny leaves from a *shiso* leaf, and add to the flower.

POMEGRANATE TEMARI SUSH

Makes 1
¼ cup vinegared rice (p 86)
¼ sheet toasted *nori*
½ Tbsp *ikura*

1. Wrap the rice in a plastic wrap, and press gently to form a tiny ball.
2. Remove the wrap, and wrap again with a sheet of *nori*.
3. Cut a crisscross score into the top, and fill the gap with *ikura*.

PERSIMMON TEMARI SUSHI

The green color represents a young fruit. The unique hull of the persimmon is imitated with *nori* and salmon *sashimi*.

POMEGRANATE TEMARI SUSHI

Ikura brims over the *nori*-wrapped ball of vinegared rice.

BOUNCING TEMARI SUSHI

Crunchy *tobiko* rice ball with "seams" of *nori* strips.

BASEBALL
Just draw the seemlines with two strips of *nori*.

BASKETBALL
Such tasty ball lunch will cheer up everyone on the match.

RUGBY BALL
A stamina-building *tobiko* rice with *shiitake* seams.

TENNIS BALL
A yellow ball made of egg *soboro*, accented with ham seams.

SOCCER BALL
You won't be blamed for "handing" this soccer ball.

Makes 5
1-1½ cups vinegared rice (p 86)

Basketball: *Mentaiko* **(chili cod roe)**
Rugby ball: *Tobiko* **(salted flying fish roe)**
Tennis ball: **Egg** *soboro* **(p 5)**
Nori, **cut into thin strips**
Simmered *shiitake* **mushroom (p 82)**
Cooked ham

Fold the rice with *tobiko*, *mentaiko* or egg *soboro* as needed, and divide into 5 portions. Wrap each in a plastic wrap, and form a ball shape. Remove the wrap, and stick on patterns made of : *nori* strips, *nori* pentagons, ham strips, and/ or strips of simmered *shiitake* mushroom.

TORTOISESHELL CAT
A good combination of sweet and salty flavors.

TABBY CAT
The body is tinted with egg *soboro*, and the pattern is made with simmered *kampyo*.

RED CAT
Crunchy *tobiko* rice with collar of ham and tail of carrot.

Makes 3
1-1½ cup vinegared rice (p 86)
Nori, **cut into shapes**
Soba **(buckwheat) noodles, fried crisp**
Cooked ham, cut into strips
Simmered *shiitake* **mushroom (p 82)**

Tortoiseshell: Simmered *kampyo* **(p 82)**
          Katsuobushi **(bonito shavings)**
          Dash soy sauce
Tabby: Egg *soboro*
     Tamagoyaki **(thick omelet -p 69)**
     Simmered *kampyo* **(p 82)**
Red: *Tobiko* **(salted flying fish roe)**
    Cooked carrot

1. Toss the rice with egg *soboro* or *tobiko*, as needed. (Make Tortoiseshell body with plain vinegared rice.)
2. Divide the rice into 3, and wrap each in a plastic wrap. Press to form an oval shape, and remove the wrap. Wrap each neck with a collar of ham strip.
3. Make features :
For Tortoiseshell Cat, moisten the *katsuobushi* with soy sauce, and make patches with it on the body. Make muzzle and tail with *shiitake*. Make ears with *kampyo*. Make eyes and mouth with *nori*. Form whiskers by thrusting fried *soba* noodle pieces into cheeks.
For Tabby Cat, make features in the same manner as for the Tortoiseshell. Make ears and tail with omelet. Make stripes with simmered *kampyo*.
For Red Cat, add ears and tail of cooked carrot.

MINIATURE DOLL COUPLE ON THE SHELL THRONES

Edible doll couples for the Doll Festival dinner. Emperor and Empress are seated on shell thrones.

Makes 1 pair
¼ **cup vinegared rice (p 86)**
Sakura dembu **(cod flakes)**
Egg *soboro* **(p 5)**
Tamagoyaki **(thick omelet - p 69)**
Cucumber peel
Cooked carrot
Party picks

1. Divide the rice into two. Make pink rice by mixing one half of the rice with *sakura dembu*, and set aside until excess moisture is absorbed. Make yellow rice by mixing the remaining rice with egg *soboro*.

2. Make Empress. Shape each into a cone. Cut a cube of omelet, and secure it with a party pick on top of the pink cone, as head. Cut cooked carrot into a thin strip, and cut a crack at one end. Thread the other end into it, and place on the body.

3. Make Emperor. Make head with a cucumber dice, and secure it with a party pick on top of the yellow cone. Thread one end of the cucumber strip in the same manner as the carrot, and place on the body.

4. Place each on an empty clam shell, set on a mound of salt.

Note: The pale pink petals are cutouts from pickled ginger slices.

MINIATURE SUSHI DOLLS

Quail egg heads top the sushi bodies, wrapped in elegant *kimonos* in this version.
Little girls will love the details such as the fried *soba* noodle used in place of wooden pick
for securing the clothes.

Makes 1 pair
½ cup vinegared rice (p 86)
2 quail eggs, boiled
Cooked ham
1 thin omelet (p 69)
Lettuce leaf
Kamaboko **(fishcake)**
Toasted *nori*
Cooked carrot
Yamagobo **pickles (pokeweed)**
Soba **(buckwheat) noodles, fried crisp**

1. Divide the rice into half portions, and form each into a short cone shape.
2. Make Empress by wrapping one cone of rice with layered ham and omelet. Secure the joint by sticking a short *soba* noodle. Push in black sesame seeds and a thin strip of vinegared ginger into an egg, to make eyes and mouth. Secure the head with a party pick, pushing through a knot of ham strip, into the body. Cut a fan shape carrot, and attach it just above the joint of *kimono*.
3. Make Emperor. Wrap the rice with a lettuce leaf, and secure the ends with a stick of fried *soba*. Make head in the same manner as Empress, and secure it with a party pick pushing through a knotted *shiitake* strip. Make scepter with *yamagobo*, and secure with fried *soba* noodle.

67

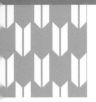 

With a pressing sushi mold, you can make several neat sushi squares at once.
Layer several shades or sandwich with your favorite fillings,
and arrange the top as desired.

LAYERED SUSHI

Tasty *tarako* (cod roe) rice and egg rice are layered and topped with *ikura*, cucumber and shredded omelet. Enjoy the combination of warm colors and flavors.

Makes 3
2½-3 cups vinegared rice (p 86)
Toasted *nori* (2½" x 7" / 6 cm x 18 cm)
***Tarako* (salted cod roe)**
Egg *soboro* (p 5)
Thin omelet
Toasted white sesame seeds
***Ikura* (salted salmon roe)**
Thinly sliced Japanese cucumber

1. Combine ⅔ of the rice with *tarako* to make pink rice. Combine the remaining rice with egg *soboro* to make yellow rice. Shred thin omelet.
2. Prepare mold. If using a wooden sushi mold, dip in water and drain to prevent rice from sticking. If using metallic baking pan, line the bottom and sides with a plastic wrap for easy unmolding.
3. Lay a half sheet of *nori* on the bottom of the mold, and spread half of the pink rice over it. Sprinkle with generous amount of white sesame seeds and spread the yellow rice. Sprinkle with sesame seeds again, then spread the pink rice. Top with the other half sheet of *nori*. Press evenly, and unmold.
4. Cut into 3, and place cucumber slices, shredded omelet, and top with *ikura*.

Note : See opposite page for step-by-step illustrations.

HOW TO MAKE PRESSED SUSHI

1

Wet wooden sushi mold to prevent rice from sticking. Dip all the parts in water 10 minutes, and drain.

A standard sushi mold measures 2½" x 7 " x 2" (6 cm x 18 cm x 5 cm) inside.

2

Set the frame on the bottom piece. If using an oblong or square baking pan, line with a plastic wrap.

3

Lay a sheet of *nori* cut to the size of the bottom. Spread half of the pink rice evenly.

4

Sprinkle sesame seeds generously. Spread the yellow rice over it, sprinkle sesame seeds again, then fill with the remaining pink rice. Top with the *nori*.

5

Press down slowly with the lid.

6

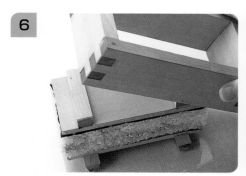

Unmold, first by removing the frame, then the other parts. Cut into appropriate portions, and decorate with toppings.

How to make thin omelet and thick omelet

Makes about 10 thin omelets
  or a 6" x 8"(15 cm x 20 cm) roll

3 eggs, beaten well
1 Tbsp sugar
Pinch of salt
Vegetable oil for greasing

Thin Omelet:
Combine beaten eggs with sugar and salt until dissolved. Do not whisk as the bubbles will remain on smooth surface of the omelet. Heat and grease a frying pan (or use nonstick pan), and pour in a small amount of the egg mixture. Cook over very low heat just until set, and turn the omelet over. Remove from heat after 5 seconds. Repeat to make about 10 sheets. Be sure to grease the pan each time. Thin omelet sheets can be kept frozen.

***Tamagoyaki* / thick omelet**
Heat a square or oblong Japanese omelet pan, and grease with a dash of vegetable oil. Pour in ⅓ of the egg mixture. Cook over very low heat until half done. Using chopsticks or a spatula, roll up tightly. Push the roll to the far end of the pan, and pour another ⅓ of the mixture. When almost done, roll the far edge towards you. Repeat to make a thick roll of omelet.

SUSHI SQUARES

SALMON SLICE : A

Smoked salmon tops sushi rice layered with aromatic *shiso* leaf. *Edamame* (young soybeans) and cooked ham are placed on a lattice, made of thin omelet strips.

SALMON SLICE : B

Stripes of cheese *kamaboko* (fishcake), ham and cucumber decorate the layered sushi squares.

Makes 3 each (For 2½" x 7" x 2"/ 6 cm x 18 cm x 5 cm mold)
2½-3 cups vinegared rice (p 86)
3-4 slices smoked salmon
***Shiso* leaves**

For A:
  Thin omelet (p 69), sliced thinly
  Cooked ham, cut into rounds
  ***Edamame* (young soybeans), boiled**
    (Thaw frozen *edamame*)
  Mayonnaise
For B:
  Cheese *kamaboko* (fishcake), cut into thin
    strips
  Cooked ham, cut into thin strips
  Cucumber peel, cut into thin strips
  Mayonnaise

1. In a mold, lay smoked salmon slices. Spread half of the rice, lay *shiso* leaves, then spread the remaining rice over them.
2. Press evenly and unmold.
3. Cut into small, bite-size pieces. Decorate the tops with thinly sliced omelet, split *edamame* beans, mayonnaise dots and tiny rounds of ham for A. For B, lay cheese *kamaboko*, ham and cucumber in a stripe pattern, and dot with mayonnaise between them.

RAINBOW SLICE

It's always fun to cut a stack of
food and unveil beautiful cut edges.

Makes 1 dozen
(For 2½" x 7" x 2"/ 6 cm x 18 cm x 5 cm mold)
2½-3 cups vinegared rice (p 86)
Toasted *nori* (2½" x 7 "/ 6 cm x 18 cm)
Sakura dembu **(cod flakes)**
Tobiko **(salted flying fish roe)**
Egg *soboro* (p 5)
Aonori **(green seaweed**
   sprinkles)
Yukari **(*shiso* sprinkles)**

1. Combine ⅕ of the rice with *sakura
dembu* to make pink rice, and set
aside. In the same manner, make
orange rice with *tobiko*, yellow rice
with egg *soboro*, green rice with
aonori, and purple rice with *yukari*.
2. Lay half sheet of *nori* on the bottom
of a mold. Spread the pink rice. Layer
the colored rice in order: orange,
yellow, green, ending with purple.
3. Top with the remaining half sheet of
nori. Press evenly, and unmold. Cut
into 6 squares. (Wipe the blade of
knife with wetted kitchen towel after
each slicing.)

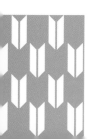

On special occasions, surprise your family or guests with specially decorated sushi "cakes" like these. They are quick to prepare, especially when you have many guests.

CELEBRATION SUSHI CAKE

Layers of salmon and egg are sandwiched with vinegared rice, then decorated with "cherries" and other morsels.

Makes 6
3 cups vinegared rice (p 86)
18 shrimp, cooked
6 cherry tomatoes
6 Tbsps salmon flakes (store-bought)
⅓ *tamagoyaki* (thick omelet - p 69), sliced
2 Tbsps *ikura* (salted salmon roe)
Lettuce leaves
Thin cucumber slices
Lemon slices

1. Line a round mold* with oversized plastic wrap. Spread half of the vinegared rice on the bottom of the mold. Layer salmon flakes, omelet, then the remaining rice. Press evenly and unmold.

2. Remove the plastic wrap and cut into 6 pieces.

3. Decorate the top of each with cut-up lettuce leaf, cucumber, shrimp, tomato and *ikura*. Use a dash of mayonnaise to secure the toppings.

* Mold size: 5"(13 cm) W x 2"(5 cm) D

PRINCESS SUSHI CAKE

Enjoy layering your favorite ingredients for a pretty party sushi like this.

For a 4"(10 cm) and a 2½"(6 cm) molds
3 cups vinegared rice(p 86)
Egg *soboro* (p 5)
***Sakura dembu* (cod flakes)**
1 thin omelet sheet (p 69)
**1 sheet toasted *nori*, cut into
   rounds**
**1 slice *kamaboko* (fishcake),
   optional**
**Japanese cucumber, sliced
   thinly**
Boiled carrot
***Edamame* (young soybeans),
   boiled**
Simmered *kampyo* (p 82)
**1 oz (30 g) *maguro* (tuna) *sashimi*,
   sliced thinly**

1. Combine ⅓ of the rice with *sakura dembu* to make pink rice, and set aside. Mix a quarter of the remaining rice with egg *soboro* to make yellow rice. Shred half amount of the thin omelet sheets, saving one for layering.
2. Line molds with an oversized plastic wrap. On the bottom of the larger mold, spread the pink rice. Layer thin omelet, *nori*, and then ⅔ of the remaining white rice. Press evenly and unmold. Repeat with the smaller mold, layering the yellow rice, *nori* and white rice. Press and unmold. Place this on the larger cake.
3. Decorate the lower layer with shredded omelet, boiled carrot, shelled *edamame*, simmered *kampyo*, and *kamaboko*. See page 56 for decorative cutting.
4. Decorate the top with fanned cucumber slices and a *sashimi* rosette.

SUSHI CUPCAKES

Once you have made vinegared rice, these savory cupcakes are so easy to prepare.
Create several versions and assort them nicely like a flower garden.

SHRIMP FLOWER CUPCAKE

Makes 1
1 cup vinegared rice (p 86)
Yukari (*shiso* **sprinkles**)
Tobiko (**salted flying fish roe**)
½ Tbsp chopped simmered *kampyo* **(p 82)**
½ Tbsp simmered carrot*
1-2 pea pods, boiled and shredded
1" (2.5 cm) cucumber, shredded
3-4 shrimp, boiled

1. Divide the rice into 3 portions.
Combine one portion with *yukari* to make
purple rice. Combine another with *tobiko*
to make orange rice. Combine the
remaining rice with the *kampyo*, carrot
and pea pods.
2. In a clear container, put purple rice,
mixed white rice, then the orange rice,
pressing flat after each addition.
3. Top with shredded cucumber and boiled
shrimp.

*Simmered Carrot
1 small carrot, chopped
1 cup *dashi* stock
2 Tbsps sugar
2 tsps soy sauce

In a small saucepan, cook carrot in *dashi* stock,
sugar and soy sauce over low heat until the
moisture is reduced. Let cool before mixing.

TOMATO FLOWER CUPCAKE

Makes 1
1 cup vinegared rice (p 86)
Egg *soboro* (p 5)
1 simmered *shiitake* mushroom (p 82), sliced
½ Tbsp simmered carrot (opposite page)
1 pea pods, boiled and shredded
1 slice cooked ham, shredded
1 cherry tomato, sliced thinly
Mustard sprouts

1. Divide the rice into 3 portions. Combine one portion with *sakura dembu* to make pink rice, and set aside. Combine another portion with egg *soboro* to make yellow rice. Combine the remaining rice with simmered *shiitake*, carrot, and pea pods until evenly mixed.
2. In a clear container, put pink rice, mixed white rice, then the yellow rice, pressing flat after each addition.
3. Top with shredded ham, and a flower of tomato petals and sprout center.

IKURA FLOWER CUPCAKE

Makes 1
1 cup vinegared rice (p 86)
Egg *soboro* (p 5)
***Aonori* (green seaweed sprinkles)**
1 simmered *shiitake* mushroom (p 82), sliced
½ Tbsp simmered carrot (opposite page)
1 pea pods, boiled and shredded
Thin egg omelet (p 69)
1 tsp *ikura* (salted salmon roe)

1. Divide the rice into 3 portions. Combine one portion with egg *soboro* to make yellow rice. Combine another with *aonori* to make green rice. Combine the remaining rice with simmered *shiitake*, carrot and pea pods.
2. Layer thin omelet sheets and shred finely.
3. In a clear container, put the yellow rice, mixed white rice, then the green rice, and press flat.
4. Top with shredded thin omelet, sliced pea pod, and *ikura*.

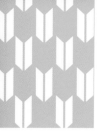

FUN SHAPES

Use cookie cutters, jelly molds or molded baking tins to make cheerful designs.
You can substitute *nori* with toasted sesame seeds, if you prefer.

POPULAR SHAPES

Makes 1 set
(for 2 medium cookie cutters)
½ cup vinegared rice (p 86)
***Sakura dembu* (cod flakes)**
***Tobiko* (salted flying fish roe)**
Toasted *nori*
Egg *soboro* (p 5)
Dash vegetable oil for greasing

1. Saving ⅔ of the rice, make 1 tsp of
pink rice with *sakura dembu*, make
yellow rice with egg *soboro*, and
orange rice with *tobiko*. Set aside.
2. Grease a cookie cutter lightly with a
dash of vegetable oil. Pack it with the
saved white rice. Unmold and wrap the
sides in a strip of *nori* cut longer
than the circumference.
3. Form a mound of rice in graded
colors. Press down lightly to secure.

CAR

Makes 1
¼ **cup vinegared rice (p 86)**
Toasted *nori*
Cooked ham
Boiled carrot
Thin omelet (p 69)
Edamame **(young soybeans), boiled**
Dash vegetable oil for greasing

1. Grease a cookie cutter with vegetable oil only lightly, and wipe off excess. Pack the rice into the cookie cutter, then unmold. Wrap the sides in *nori*, cut longer than the circumference.
2. Cut the car shape of the omelet, and lay on the rice. Cut ham, carrot and *edamame* as shown, and place on the omelet.

DUCK COUPLE

Makes 1 pair
½ **cup vinegared rice (p 86)**
Sakura dembu **(cod flakes)**
Toasted *nori*
Thin omelet (p 69)
Edamame **(young soybeans), boiled**
Boiled carrot
Cooked ham
Toasted white and black sesame seeds
Dash vegetable oil for greasing

1. Mix half of the rice with *sakura dembu* to make pink rice, and set aside.
2. Pack the remaining rice into a greased cookie cutter, then unmold. Wrap the sides in *nori* cut longer than the circumference.
3. Make toppings:
For male duck, place thin omelet cut into body and beak shapes. Press the white sesame seeds onto body. Place *edamame*, carrot and a black sesame seed as shown.
For female duck, pack the pink rice into the cookie cutter, then unmold. Place ham, *edamame*, omelet (beak) and a black sesame seed as shown.

LANDSCAPE

Layers of blooming hills represent the
spring season.

ONION PATCH

Early spring scenery with fresh sprouts
waving in a soft wind.

BUTTERFLY

A good companion to the spring field.
Tiny broccoli sprout leaves can make
an effective pattern.

CAMELLIA

Kids love this kind of simple floral
pattern, which adds a sense of season to your table.

Makes 1 each
1 cup vinegared rice (p 86)
Toasted *nori*
Thin omelet (p 69)
Boiled carrot
Cucumber, sliced paper thin
***Edamame* (young soybeans), boiled**
***Sakura dembu* (cod flakes)**
Sesame seed sprinkles
Broccoli sprouts
Dash vegetable oil for greasing

1. Grease cookie cutter(s) with oil, and wipe off. Pack the rice into the cutter, then unmold. Wrap the sides in a strip of *nori* cut longer than the circumference.
2. Make toppings:
For Landscape, cut out omelet, carrot and ham with a cutter, and place sesame sprinkles.
For Butterfly, spread *sakura dembu* on the rice, and cut ham, omelet into wing shapes. Use thinly cut carrot sticks for feelers.
For Onion Patch, place omelet on arranged half slices of cucumber, and place ham "dots" in a row.
For Camellia, place cut out and layered ham slices, and add omelet strips and carrot dots between them. Add split *edamame* at the bottom.

CHRISTMAS TREE

Aonori sprinkles make the fir leaves while carrot, ham and egg twinkle among them.

Makes 1
¼ cup vinegared rice (p 86)
Toasted *nori*
Aonori (green seaweed sprinkles)
Boiled carrot, chopped
Cooked ham, chopped
Thin omelet (p 69), chopped
Dash vegetable oil for greasing

1. Grease the cookie cutter and wipe off excess. Pack the rice into the cutter, then unmold. Wrap the sides in a strip of *nori*, cut longer than the circumference.
2. Sprinkle *aonori* generously over the top, and arrange carrot, ham and omelet bits.

CHRISTMASTIME

STAR

You can replace the topping with red cheddar cheese, Parma ham and dill pickles.

Makes 1
¼ cup vinegared rice (p 86)
Toasted *nori*
Boiled carrot
Cooked ham
Thin omelet (p 69)
Dash vegetable oil for greasing

1. Grease the cookie cutter and wipe off. Pack the rice into the cutter, then unmold. Wrap the sides in a strip of *nori*, cut longer than the circumference.
2. Cut out ham and omelet. Cut carrot into thin sticks, and arrange on the rice.

INARI SUSHI

Inari sushi is a sweetly seasoned *tofu* pouch stuffed with vinegared rice, which is usually a simple, oblong piece. Here is a variety of little fun faces for you to enjoy, since *inari* sushi tastes great when made in smaller sizes.

FOX

Makes 2
1 cup vinegared rice (p 86)
2 *inari* pouches (p 82, or
   store-bought seasoned *abura-age* /fried *tofu*)
Simmered *shiitake* mushroom (p 82)
Boiled carrot
Toasted *nori*

1. Press the rice in your hand to shape a ball. Put it into the seasoned *inari* pouch, filling the bottom half only. Fold back the opening, then fold back the sides to form a fox's face.
2. Make eyes with *shiitake*, nose with carrot, and whiskers with *nori*, all cut into thin strips. Position them by pressing onto the sushi. The moisture of the pouches will keep them from falling off.

BEAR

Makes 2
1 cup vinegared rice (p 86)
2 *inari* pouches (p 82, or
   store-bought seasoned *abura-age* /fried *tofu*)
Simmered *shiitake* mushroom (p 82)
2 boiled sugar peas

1. Press the rice in your hand to shape a ball. Put into the seasoned *inari* pouch.
2. Gather the opening edges to form muzzle, and secure it with a wooden pick penetrating through a sugar pea.

ELEPHANT

Makes 2
1 cup vinegared rice (p 86)
2 *inari* pouches (p 82, or
   store-bought seasoned *abura-age* /fried *tofu*)
Simmered *shiitake* mushroom (p 82)

1. When opening the pouch, leave the corners unopen to form ears.
2. Press half of the rice in your hand to shape a ball. Put it into the seasoned *inari* pouch. Fold back the sides forming long nose and stand-up ears.
3. Put *shiitake* cut into small pieces as eyes.

RACCOON

Makes 2

1 cup vinegared rice (p 86)
2 *inari* pouches (p 82, or
 store-bought seasoned *abura-age* /fried *tofu*)
Thin omelet (p 69)
Toasted *nori*
Simmered *shiitake* mushroom (p 82)

1. Reverse the seasoned pouch so the rough skin shows. Press half of the rice in your hand to shape a ball. Put into the seasoned *inari* pouch, filling only half of it. Form a raccoon face by folding down the edges.
2. Cut a bean shape out of thin omelet, and stick to the face. Add *shiitake* cut into small pieces, as eyes.

KITTEN

Makes 2

1 cup vinegared rice (p 86)
2 *inari* pouches (p 82, or store-bought seasoned *abura-age* /fried *tofu*)
Simmered *shiitake* mushroom (p 82)
Simmered *kampyo* (p 82)

1. Press half of the rice in your hand to shape an oblong ball. Put into seasoned *inari* pouch, filling only half of it. Fold it in half to form a rectangle.
2. Stick *nori* cut into thin strips. Bind the sushi with simmered *kampyo*, resembling a cuff or scarf.

Makes 2

1 cup vinegared rice (p 86)
2 *inari* pouches (p 82, or
 store-bought seasoned *abura-age* /fried *tofu*)
Egg *soboro* (p 5)
Simmered *shiitake* mushroom (p 82)
Boiled carrot
4 boiled sugar peas

1. Combine the rice with ample egg *soboro* carefully to make yellow rice.
2. Fold the opening of the *inari* pouch inside, and put in half of the rice.
3. Place thinly cut *shiitake* for the line, peas for eyes, and carrot for mouth.

MONKEY

DINOSAUR NEST

Makes 1
½ cup vinegared rice (p 86)
1 *inari* pouch (below, or
   store-bought seasoned *abura-age* /
   fried *tofu*)
Egg *soboro* (p 5)
Thin omelet (p 69), shredded

1. Combine the rice with egg *soboro* to make yellow rice.
2. Fold the opening of the *inari* pouch inside, and put the shredded omelets. Form the yellow rice into tiny "eggs", and place on the omelet shreds.

Note: Squeeze *inari* pouches lightly before filling with the rice. Too much moisture may make the rice soggy and loose.

INARI POUCHES
Commercial *inari* sushi pouches are available at many Asian markets.

Makes a dozen
6 *abura-age* (fried *tofu*)
1 cup *dashi* stock
7 Tbsps sugar
5 Tbsps soy sauce
1 Tbsp *mirin* (or rice wine)
For a hidden flavor, add 2 tsps of honey to the above.

1. Lay *abura-age* on a board, cover with a plastic wrap, and roll with a rolling pin. This breaks the inside tissue and makes opening easy.
2. Pour over ample boiling water to remove excess oil. Cut into halves, and open the pouches.
3. In a saucepan, heat *dashi* stock, sugar, soy sauce and *mirin* to a boil. Squeeze the prepared pouches and add to the pan. Lower the heat, and simmer about 15 minutes until the liquid is almost gone. Remove from heat and let cool in the pan.

SIMMERED KAMPYO (GOURD STRIPS)
A most common filling for rolled sushi.

Makes 7 oz (200 g)
⅔ oz (20 g) *kampyo* (dried)
1 tsp salt
1 cup *dashi* stock
4 Tbsps sugar
4 Tbsps soy sauce

1. Soak *kampyo* in water for 3-5 minutes. Drain most of the water, and rub *kampyo* with salt grains for a minute until supple.Rinse off salt. Cook in ample boiling water until soft, for 15-20 minutes. Cut into desired lengths.
2. Heat *dashi* stock, sugar and soy sauce to a boil, and simmer *kampyo* over low heat about 15 minutes until the sauce is absorbed.

SIMMERED *SHIITAKE* MUSHROOMS
Other than using for making shapes, mix them into the rice for *inari* sushi for a better flavor.

Makes 6
6 medium dried *shiitake* mushrooms
1 cup from *shiitake* soaking water
4 Tbsps sugar
4 Tbsps soy sauce

1. Soften *shiitake* in water until soft. Drain and trim off stems.
2. Heat the soaking water, sugar and soy sauce to a boil. Add *shiitake* and simmer until the sauce is absorbed.

SHOE

Makes 1
½ **cup vinegared rice (p 86)**
**1 *inari* pouch (p 82, or
store-bought seasoned *abura-age* /
fried *tofu*)**
Thin omelet (p 69), shredded

1. Press the rice gently in your hand to form an oval. Put it in the *inari* pouch. Fold in one end of the pouch, and bring the sides to the center; secure with a wooden pick.
2. Cut 2 pieces of egg shoe lace. Tie a bow with a longer lace, and cut the other in two. Place them over the joint.

ZAURUS

Makes 2
1 cup vinegared rice (p 86)
**2 *inari* pouches (p 82, or
store-bought seasoned *abura-age* /
fried *tofu*)**
***Kamaboko* (fishcake)**
Toasted *nori*

1. Press the rice gently in your hand to form a ball. Put it in the *inari* pouch, and form a triangle by folding the corners down.
2. Make a zigzag cut into *kamaboko*. Slit the bottom of the pouch, and insert *kamaboko*. Cut 4 eyes out of *kamaboko*. Cut *nori* into fine threads, and press them onto the sushi.

Wiener Flower
Slice a precooked cocktail wiener short. Trim away ends. Make a deep crisscross slit twice. Microwave until the skin shrinks and "petals" open. Insert a broccoli floret into the center.

Carrot Glace
Slice carrot, and then cut out shapes. Put them in a saucepan, and add water to cover. Add butter and sugar. Cook over low heat until the liquid is gone.

Cauliflower Sheep
Boil cauliflower in salty water only briefly. Make head with a boiled carrot, and thrust into cauliflower. Attach mouth of radish peel, eye(s) of *nori*. Insert legs of deep-fried *soba* (buckwheat) noodle.

Newborn Chick
Cook quail egg rolling in gently boiling water to keep the yolk at the center. Cut zigzag incision around the middle of the egg, and remove half of the egg white. Stick black sesame seeds for eyes, and a carrot piece for beak.

Egg Cherries
Dissolve little amount of red food color in water. Soak 2 hard-boiled quail eggs until evenly colored. Insert a V-shaped parsley stem ends into eggs.

Hamburger Pineapple
Form a tiny hamburger, and cook well. Using a wooden pick, draw lines of ketchup. Cut a pea pod into leaf shape, and attach to the hamburger.

Hotdog Octopus

Cut a precooked wiener in half. Make deep slits into the cut edge. Microwave until the skin shrinks and the edges curl. Stick sesame seeds for eyes, boiled carrot piece for mouth, and tie cooked spaghetti for headband.

Pepper Flowers

Slice bell pepper into ⅜" (1 cm) rings. Seed and place in a greased frying pan. Drop quail eggs into each ring, and cook until done. Sprinkle salt.

Broccoli Monster

Cook broccoli only briefly. Make dots with *kamaboko*, and stick into broccoli floret using deep-fried *soba* (buckwheat) noodles. Make mouth with boiled carrot, and attach with mayonnaise.

Tomato King

Make short slits into cherry tomato, using a pointed knife. Insert black sesame seeds for eyes.

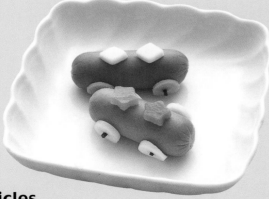

Hotdog Vehicles

Make wheels with cheese and ham. Attach them to cooked cocktail wieners using deep-fried *soba* (buckwheat) noodle. Cut out shapes from cheese and carrot, and place on top of the vehicles.

Egg Cup

Make a zigzag incision around hard-boiled egg, and pull apart. Combine egg yolk with mayonnaise, chopped parsley, salt and pepper, and then fill the cup again. Decorate with cut-out carrot and ham.

MAKING VINEGARED RICE

WASHING RICE

If using prewashed rice, omit the washing process, but be sure to use a reduced cup for rice and water measurement. In either case, use the same amount of rice and water to cook.

1. Place measured rice in a large bowl. Add water to cover, and quickly rub the grains between your palms. Repeat quickly, and discard water immediately. This way the smell of the bran is removed.

2. Add water again and repeat, this time taking more time. Repeat several times until water runs almost clear.

COOKING RICE

A rice cooker cooks perfect rice without effort, and keeps the rice warm until actual use. It is worth investing, but you can cook the rice in a pot as well with a little attention.

Rice Cooker

1. Place rinsed and drained rice in the inner pot of the cooker. Add water up to the appropriate marking line of the pot. Let rice soak 30 minutes, or turn on immediately.

2. When cooking is over, it automatically switches to keep-warm mode. Using the attached paddle, fluff rice lightly.

Note: The ratio of rice to water, and to seasonings depends on the grains. Generally, if cooking very small amount of rice, more water is needed than cooking a large batch. Check with to the table on the opposite page for the right proportions.

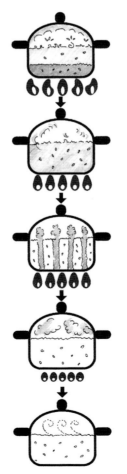

Pot or Pan

1
Use a medium pot or pan with a heavy bottom and tight lid. Place measured and rinsed rice in the pot. Add appropriate amount of water. Cover and cook 5-6 minutes over very high heat, until boiling.

2
Reduce heat to medium high, and cook 1 minute. Be careful not to boil over.

3
Reduce heat to medium, and cook 7-8 minutes.

4
Reduce heat to very low, and cook for 15 minutes. Keep covered.

5
Turn off heat, and let steam 10 minutes, covered.

Rice Cooking Table

cup: American cup (240 ml)   Add 2"(5 cm) square *kombu* to all.

DESIRED VINEGARED RICE	TO COOK		TO SEASON		
	Raw Rice	Water	Vinegar	Sugar	Salt
2½ cups	1 cup	1¼ cups	2 Tbsps	½ Tbsp	1 tsp
5 cups	2 cups	2-2¼ cups	3½ Tbsps	1 Tbsp	1½ tsps
7½ cups	3 cups	3-3¼ cups	5 Tbsps	1½ Tbsps	2 tsps
10 cups	4 cups	4-4¼ cups	7 Tbsps	2 Tbsps	1 Tbsp

- 2 cups of raw rice will make 2 rolls of basic Hana Sushi.
- Use about 100~120 % amount of water to uncooked rice, depending on the condition of the rice used. For sushi making, less cooking water is required than usual, because some vinegar will be added later.
- The rice increases by 130 % in weight when cooked.

SEASONING RICE

1
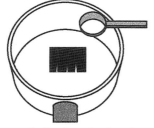

Make several slits into the *kombu* to draw out the flavor fast. Put it in a small saucepan with the vinegar, sugar and salt. Stir and cook until they dissolve. Just before the mixture reaches the boiling point, remove from heat, and discard the *kombu*.

2

Wet *hangiri* (sushi barrel) or shallow container with vinegared water lightly. Add all the cooked rice at once.

3

Swirl the vinegar mixture over the rice, using a rice paddle to distribute evenly.

4

Immediately toss the rice using the paddle, fluffing as if cutting the lumps horizontally. When the vinegar mixture is almost distributed evenly, start cooling the rice with a fan.

5

Keep fanning, constantly turning over the rice until it emits no steam and absorbs the flavor. Fanning gives a shiny look to the finished rice.

6

Cover with a damp cloth until use. Shape the rice before it becomes too cold.

FREQUENTLY ASKED QUESTIONS

Which rice to choose?

Take Japanese or short to medium grain rice. Long grain or Chinese rice will not become sticky enough for sushi when cooked. Ask for sushi rice. It is advisable to ask a local sushi chef which brands to purchase.

Which bamboo mat to choose?

Sushi rolling mat comes in various sizes; from large one (12" × 11", 30 cm × 27 cm) for thick rolls to small one that is half in length, for thin rolls. Choose a large bamboo mat as it is versatile. A cookie sheet is a good substitute for thin rolls.

Wrong side of bamboo mat?

Lay smooth side up when rolling sushi for a smoother finish. Place *nori* directly over it to make *nori* rolls while it is necessary to cover the mat with plastic wrap when making *uramaki*, or inside-out rolls. After use, be sure to rinse the mat immediately and let dry completely.

Which side of nori?

Nori sheet has smooth side and rough side. Be careful so that the smooth and shiny side shows when completed. Lay smooth side down when rolling.

Rice sticks to fingers!

Dip your fingertips in vinegared water when touching or spreading rice. A wetted tablespoon may do the work more easily to spread rice evenly.

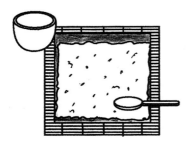

Spread rice evenly, using back of spoon.

Too much fillings?

When the *nori* seems to be too small to hold the fillings, reduce the thickness of the rice that is spread over it. If it does not solve the problem, do not cram, and make a bigger roll by adding an extra sheet of *nori* to cover.

Spread evenly and thinly. Thick or uneven layer of rice will deform the design.

Too loose fillings?

If a roll loses its shape when picked up with your fingers, it is too loosely stuffed. Before sealing the roll, press the roll by tucking the bottom edge of the roll into the far edge of the rice firmly with the bamboo mat. Also, be sure to press the side edges to flatten before unrolling the mat.

Tough nori to cut!

It is difficult to cut the *nori* right after rolling. It is best to wait 20-30 minutes until it softens, putting seam side

Knife sticks to rice!

To make the cut edges neat, wet the blade with water or wipe it with wet kitchen towel after each slicing. One roll is usually cut into 8 slices.

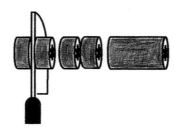

Cut in half, then into quarters.

The nori shrinks!

Toasted *nori* tends to shrink when absorbing moisture, and sometimes the rolls open up. Triangular or square rolls may turn into round roll after a while. Let stand 10-20 minutes, and reshape them using a rolling mat.

Can sushi keep refrigerated?

The vinegared rice has the potential to become tough when refrigerated. Keep sushi in a cool place as the vinegar is a natural preservative. If you keep it in a refrigerator, stand at least 1 hour at room temperature before serving.

What is dashi?

Dashi stock is one of the most common stocks for Japanese cuisine. It is made of *kombu* kelp and dried bonito flakes, but there are good substitutes sold in granules such as *dashi-no-moto*.

What is kampyo?

Kampyo is dried gourd shavings. It is used as one of the fillings for sushi rolls. To soften *kampyo*, wash and then rub with ample amount of salt. Rinse in water, and cook (see p 82). It is available in 1 oz (30 g) packets.

What is shiso?

Perilla leaves in green or purple red color. This herb is related to the mint family and has a pleasant aroma. Green *shiso* is mainly used for sushi or as a condiment for *sashimi* platters while red *shiso* is often added to pickled vegetables to add flavor and color.